Maufe, Morphew and Morffew.
A brief History, from the Norman invasion to the present day

Peter Morffew

Cover image. The green wax seal of Simon Malfe, (Maufe). Circa 1150.

**Maufe, Morphew and Morffew.
A brief History, from the Norman
invasion to the present day**

Copyright 2020 Peter G. Morffew
Published by Peter G. Morffew
Cover design by Peter Morffew

Contents

About Peter Morffew	4	4
About this book	6	6
Preface	8	8
The names and their spellings.	9	9
Demographics.	16	— 17
In the beginning. Vikings; their colonisation of Northern France.	19	— 20
1066. The Norman Invasion	21	— 23
11th Century	25	— 27
12th Century	29	— 31
13th Century	34	— 36
14th Century	55	— 58
15th Century	71	— 75
16th Century	86	— 92
17th Century	96	— 103
Morphews in America	109	— 116
18th Century	115	— 122
Morphews in America	130	— 138
19th Century	134	— 142
Morphews in America	156	— 165
Morphews in Canada	162	— 171
Morffews	163	— 173
20th Century	175	— 185
Maufes	178	— 187
Morphews in America	197	— 207
Morphews in Canada	207	— 217
Morphews in Australia	211	— 221
Morffews	215	— 226
21st Century	222	— 233
In Conclusion	223	— 234
An Historical coincidence?	229	— 241
Bibliography	232	— 244

Handwritten annotations:
- Morphews of the 19th century who served in the British Army 162
- Morphews in S.A. 172
- Morphews in Australia 180
- Morphews in America 183
- ww post 1919. 214
- morphew military served pre 1919 195
- US served in WWI 209

About Peter Morffew

Peter Morffew was born at Dulwich London in 1956. He attended Latton Bush Comprehensive school where Mr Sharky, the history teacher helped nurture Peters keen interest in history, both British and foreign history.
After leaving school Peter served in the British Army. Peter was posted to 3rd Battalion Queens Regiment which was originally a Sussex Regiment. This was when some one showed an interest in his surname. The Battalion had done a tour of Cyprus as UN peace keepers and he was asked if the name was anything to do with Morphou Gate, the border crossing between Turkish occupied Cyprus in the north and Greek Cyprus in the south, but Peter didn't have an answer. Since then Peter has been asked numerous questions about the origin of his name but has never been able to give a definite answer.
Peter started tracing his family tree and managed to find his ancestors dating back to the mid 16th century. He also came across a record of a John Morphew renting a room at Winchester in 1487. This inspired Peter to find possible relatives from an earlier date. Reading from various sources Peter was unable to find any Morphews pre 1487,
Internet resources helped, especially the brief document by Nils Visser-Huizen, a Dutch History teacher and Zoe Heukels-Morffew who carried out some research of the Morffew name. Peter followed up their research and information from the Middle Ages. This indicated a link between the name Maufe and Morphew. Searching the internet for Maufe instead of Morphew reaped results but there was still a gap when the transition from Maufe to Morphew or Morphewe

happened. This gap was narrowed down to the 15th century. Reading as much as possible about this era Peter felt he found a connection. There was not an obvious time or moment when the name changed but the Duke of Buckingham's Rebellion seemed to be the moment.

This moment in English history that has only been studied in depth by a few British historians making it that much harder to search for that moment that will pinpoint where and when the transition took place.

About this book

This book has been over a decade in the writing. It follows my previous study that attempted to trace the origin of the Morphews and Morffews. Reading about the Norman invasion, the Crusades and Tudor England only raised more questions than answers.

Recent searching on the internet has revealled information that has connected some loose ends.

Tracing the Maufé ancestral path after the Norman invasion to the Wars of the Roses where it appears the name changed from Maufé, Maufe, Maufee and Morfe to Morfey, Morphey, Morphewe and Morphew. Then in the late 18th century Morphew changed to Morffew for no apparent reason.

This book also looks at the Morphews and Morffews who emigrated to America, Canada and Australia in the 17th, 18th and 19th centuries.

I have written extracts as they appear in the records including the spelling of the names and places, but added the present day spelling of towns and villages in brackets.

Prominent individuals who had tentative connections with the Maufe's and Morphew's in the various records have potted biographies showing how they relate to the individual ancestors and events.

This book is not intended to be a genealogical research tool, but I have recorded as many Morphews and Morffews as I possibly can to show the change in the names at various dates and places.

Historical events are also included to show how they affected the Maufe's and Morphews.

Even though this book is primarily about the Maufe, Morphew and Morffew families I have included the Morphey and Morfy names from Sussex, Surrey,

Suffolk and Norfolk.

This book has used various sources from published books and the internet.

The information has been laid out chronologically by each century to help piece together the lives of individuals.

There are listings of births or baptism's and in some cases burials. Military service has also been listed where available but some names are missing which I apologise for.

Preface

Over the years I have been asked numerous times about the origin of my name, (Morffew). It has been speculated that Morffew was connected to Morphou in Northern Cyprus, a Crusading Baronage created by the King of Jerusalem or the Huguenots of France. It is a name that is prone to being miss-spelt in various ways. I was inspired to embark on a journey to find the source of my name, its history and to trace my own ancestry. Reputable ancestral and heraldric lists link the Morphew, Morffew and Maufe names but I wondered why? Unravelling the story and history has been long and interesting, delving in to history dating back to the Norman invasion. My first publication, 'A brief history of the Morphew and Morffew names' outlined the history of the relative periods and the events that might have brought the name changes.

Reading through material in published books, documents on the internet and records that relate to the Crusades, Norman England, Tudor England and later I built up a picture of the history about the various people over the centuries.

The earliest record I found of a Morffew is in 1796 at Kingston on Thames. The earliest record I have come across of the Morphew name dates back to 1489, not long after Englands 'Wars of the Roses'. The earliest record of the Maufe name is on the Battel Abbey Roll, attributed to commemorate the Normans at the Battle of Hastings where a Mengel (Menyle) et Maufe is listed along with other names.

I am indebted to the extensive work done by Zoe Heukels-Morffew & Nils Visser-Huizen. Also by James Murphey on his very good informative work of Morphews in America, this has been immensley invaluable.

The names and their Spellings

"MAUFEE: La Mauffe is a place in the arrondissement of St. Lo, in Normandy. The family were in Sussex at an early period. The name still exists as Morfee and Morphew. On adjacent tombstones at Woodchurch, co. Kent, it is spelt both Morfee and Morfeet."
Patronymica Britannica (1860) by Mark Antony Lower

The above paragraph from the Patronymica Britannica briefly out lines the name changes from Maufee, Morfee and finally to Morphew. It shows the original name became ramified over time. It makes you wonder why these changes took place or when. How they came about and how their lives were woven in to history.

The name Maufee can be found in the Dictionnaire du Moyen Français where it is also written as Malfe, meaning 'Demon'.

The Dictionnaire L'Ancienne Langue Française, (Dictionary of Ancient French Language). A dictionary written in the 19th century by Frederic Godefroy lists ancient French words from the 9th to the 15th century, the listing includes words of different French dialects. Under Maufee this word is also spelt as Malfé, Maufé, Mauffé, Maufei, Maffe Maffet, Malfeir, Maufie, Maufel, Malfait, Mauffait, Malfee and Malfei.

All of these different spellings had the same definition in different regions of Medieval France, 'Demon'.

The Anglo Norman Dictionary and Dictionary of Middle French 1330-1500 also have various spellings associated with Maufé, they include Malfé, Malfed, Malfee, Malfet, Malfié, Maufee, Maufié, Malfeu, Malfet and Malfait. The Anglo Norman Dictionary gives a definition referring to Demon or Evil Spirit.

[handwritten note: Moores in Provence and carried out raids in the N France from Iberia (Spain)]

The Dictionary of Middle French 1300-1500 is more specific and says it refers to a misdeed or wicked act waiting for you. It is also a legal definition refering to an assault or injury.

Various texts use the name Maufé for the Saracens (Sarrazin) or a monster. A French phrase 'la gent Maufé' referes to a Muslim in the Middle Ages

In Normandy there is the small commune of la Meauffe in la Manche, Normandy, France. La Meauffe was up until the start of the 19th century spelt La Mauffe. There are records of a Pierre de la Meauffe joining the First Crusade, also a Thomas de la Meauffe dying before 1270 which suggests that maybe la Meauffe was derived from these long dead knights. La Meauffe is on the river, la Vire which flows through Saint Lo and meanders across the Normandy countryside to the English Channel.

In England after the Norman invasion Maufe was of a single family holding land in Sussex and Northamptonshire, two counties some distance apart. Later they also held land in Suffolk, Huntingdonshire (Cambridgeshire) and Surrey again some distance apart.

During the middle ages the language of the English Court and law was Norman French. Medieval Latin was used by the church and in learning but not all those involved in the church could write or speak Latin fluently, Thomas Becket, the Arch Bishop Of Canterbury was one in particular. Anglo-Saxon was still spoken by many after the Norman Invasion. Records in the Middle Ages written by the Alderman included different nationalities, known then as strangers. They included Burgundians, Flemish, Savoyards, Lombards (Italians) and French. The Alderman recorded their names as pronounced, in many cases without a translator.

Priests were invited to England from the various parts of Europe. One order was the Cluniac's, favoured by William I. also the Pope sent his own Priests to England as ambassadors to the churches and Monarchs.

Different regional accents would have caused some confusion with the pronunciation of place and individual names, just as they do today. An example is the Land held at Chalvington by the Maufe family in Sussex. This was Chanton in traditional Anglo Saxon, (Harold Godwinson, later King Harold II owned land a short distance away at Ripe (Rype) before the Norman invasion. In the Domesday Book Chalvington was written as Calvintone or Cavetone.

A Norman Lord, l'Aigle took over King Harolds land at Ripe after the Norman invasion. L'Aigle was abbreviated to Laigle then became latinised and written as Aquila, in Staffordshire this was written as Aquilate. During the First Crusade there was the language difference between the northern and southern French Crusaders, they spoke a different French language, Langues d'oil and Languedoc (Occitan) which caused confusion and some animosity, to add confusion Norman was different to either of these French languages.

In Medieval England the Maufé name was also spelt as Maufe, Malfey, Malfe, Malfet, Malfeth, Maufee, Maffay and Maufai in various records (Rolls).

A Morfe Forest in Shropshire and Worcestershire is recorded. It was preambled in 1300 when it was refered to as the 'Royal Morfe Forest'. It was a popular forest for hunting by the monarchs up to the late Middle Ages. Morfe Forest was preambled again in the 18th century and the name on the schematic map was written as Morfé. Close by is Morphe Lane and Morphe Farm. During the Reign of Edward I a Henry de Morf is recorded as the warden of Morf Forest.

After the Late Middle Ages when Middle English (Chauser English) was used spelling started to be standardised.

During the Middle Ages nick names were extensively used, by nobility and less prominent individuals.

The Duke of Suffolk was refered to as 'Jachanapes' which was a slang name for a monkey. The Duke of Suffolk's heraldric badge was an Apes Clog, a wooden block with a chain. Jakanape came to refer to an impertinent or conceted person.

Other known nick names were Duke Robert the Devil, Hugh d'Avranches the Fat who was 1st Earl of Chester, Daniel Finch, 8th Earl of Winchelsea was refered to as 'dismal'. More complimentary nick names were Humphrey, Duke of Gloucester who was said to be 'The Good Duke and 'The Protector'.

It makes you wonder if Maufé and Morphew were originally nick names.

In Northern Cyprus was the town Morphou. This name has changed only recently but during the Middle Ages when the Crusading Monarchs ruled Cyrpus there was a baronage title of 'Morphou' which was given to many nobles over the centuries. Jean de Morphou was one of the richest barons in Cyrpus in his life time. The barons recruited mercenaries, Burgandians were very popular.

The Morphou region of Cyprus was ideal for growing sugar and was exported across Europe. It was recognised by the molded blocks of sugar in the shape of a bell. Near Morphou the Knights Templars refined raw cane in to sugar. With their extensive network through out Europe during the Middle Ages Morphou become well known.

The reformation in 1535 under Henry VIII dispensed with Latin and entries in Parish Records were written in New English, (Tudor English). The new bible introduced by Henry VIII was written the same way so many could read and understand it. Under the reign of Mary I; an English Catholic monarch, some parish records reverted to using Latin until the end of her reign. Having said that Latin was still used in legal documents and the military where a common language was needed when armies were in alliance and Latin allowed communication between the commanders up until the 19th century.

Parish records were introduced in 1535 by Henry VIII to record of Births, Marriages and Deaths. Those writing the records might not be familiar with the regional accent and wrote the name as they were visualised and Maufe changed to Maufee, Mauphee, Morphew, Morphue Morphewe, Morphe, Morphen and Morfew. Morphews lived predominantly in Surrey, Norfolk and Suffolk during the 15th and 16th centruries. Morphews were some of the earliest settlers in America working on the tobacco plantations. Some of the early settlers in the British Colonies had the name spelt Murphew as well as Morphew.

As spelling became standardised over time, the silent 'e' was dropped. The name Morphew continues to this day in the US, Britain, Australia, etc.

Morphew changed to Morffew at the end of the 18th century. Today this causes some confusion when many people write Morffew as Morphew or even Morffen, amongst others.

It might be of coincidence that the name Morphew is spelt the same as the medieval generic term for a skin affliction and the blemish associated with scurvy. The spelling of this medieval medical term transformed over the centuries and seemed to mirror the name transformation.

Medieval Latin spelling for the medical term was Morphea, in modern Latin it is spelt Morphue. Already there is a similarity with the name Maufe. In Italian it is spelt Morphea, again a very similar pronunciation of Maufe or Maufee.

The Oxford English Dictionary states Morphew refers to any various skin disease characterised by localised or generalised discolouration of skin and was called either "Black Morphew" or "White Morphew". The earliest use is found in Lanfrancs Science of Cirurgie. In Anglo-Norman and Middle French is written as Morphé. Old French it is written as Morfoies for the plural and Morphee, Morphea or Morphée. These could be taken from the Greek Morphia meaning unsightliness or ugliness.

The Greek source is feasible. Greek was spoken in Byzanium during the middle ages. Some of those on the First Crusade were known to be speak Greek and conversed in Greek to negotiate the crossing at Constantinople, (Istanbul).

During the late middle ages and through the 16th century, (The Rennaisance Period) there was an interest in studying Greek. Queen Elizabeth was considered well versed in Greek and educated individuals read Greek literature. Later in the 16th century Greek was part of the grammar school curriculum during the reformation. Learning Greek was partly in response to the Latin used by the Catholic Church.

A Medicinal shopping list dated 1544 13 June mentions the ailment morphew, 'pills for my lord Lennox; (Matthew Stewart, 4th Earl of Lennox), 8d.; aqua pro oculis for my lord, 12d. 21 Nov., centaure, etc., 4d. 5 Feb., aqua composita, a vial, 4d.; "wormesede [ounce]j.," 12d. 2 April, spermaceti [ounce]s., 12d. 26 July, "2 plasters pro scapulis," 2s. 8d.; an ointment ex diversis ut patet," 16d. 28 May, "treacle for her monkey," 8d.; "2 glasses with aqua lactis virginis for the morphew,...........'.

Another reference to the medical condition Morphew is in a list of remedies from the 17th century. Aqua Bryony, the principal ingredient was Bryony, a very poisonous plant. It was made in to a liquid hence the "Aqua" prefix. Culpeper suggested that it 'cleanseth the skin wonderfully from all black and blue spots, freckles, morphew, leprosy, foul scars, and other deformity whatsoever'.

In the Middle Ages there were itinerant quacks known as 'Leeches'. They would read out their list known as 'baans'. One baan referes to various medical conditions including 'morphew' which explains that it makes a person faint and greatly discoloured his visage.

Because of the medical condition of morphew might have been offensive possibly the 'E' was added at the end, the Morphewe name being created to distinguish it from the medical term.

The spelling of this medical term stayed the same until the mid 19th century when it replaced with more specific medical names, but the name Morphew lives on.

It is interesting to note that the name Morfu can be found in Italy and Argentina. Argentina encouraged immigration from Italy and Italian communities can be found in Beunos Aires with predominant Italian neighbourhoods.

Demographics

The geographical spread of the Maufe's, Morphew's and Morffews since 1066 is interesting. Found predominatly in the southern counties of England through the Middle Ages. In the 17th century some settled in the American colony of Virginia and later in Maryland and Carolina.

In the 19th century Morffews and Morphews migrated to Australia and Canada.

In the 11th century the Maufe's concentrated in Northamptonshire and Sussex initially.

The Domes Day Book of 1086 shows they held land in several places in Northamptonshire, at Woodford, Kingsthorpe near Hemington and Arnston.

They later held land in Huntingdonshire, (Cambridgeshire). The Sussex land was to become extensive, this included Possingworth, Ripe, Hoathey, Eastborne. By the 13th century the land in Northamptonshire was inheirted by William Maufe four daughters and passed down in their families.

The name changed from Maufe or Maufee to Morphew in the late 15th century and so did the demographics.

In the 16th century when parish records started Morphews were mainly found in Norfolk and Surrey. In Norfolk they lived around Pulham and in Surrey Bletchingley and Suffolk mainly in Hoxne.

At the turn of the 17th century Morphews were living in South Norfolk in a small area that included several villages at Pulham, Tibenham, Dickleburgh and Thorpe Abbotts. These villages are just a few miles apart and not far from the Manor of the Duke of Norfolk.

Morphews living in Surrey still lived in Bletchingley but also Merstham just a few miles away.

In the 17th century Morphews were recorded in Sussex at Mayfield and later Burwash, two main areas of the

iron industry in the Weald at the time.
As the century progressed the Morphews branched out to Denton in Norfolk, Godstone in Surrey and Rotherfield in Sussex where the Iron industry really took off with blast furnaces'.
It was at this time Morphews migrated to the American colonies at Virginia and Cape Cod.
Morphews in the 18th century could be found in the same small cluster in Norfolk but also at Ketteringham, Diss and Shimpling.
In Surrey Morphews still lived in Merstham but later in the century some moved to Kingston, (Kingston upon Thames).
In Sussex the iron industry dictated where Morphews could be found. This was a time when the industry was at full tilt employing individuals in the foundries, also tree felling to make the charcoal for the furnaces.
Morphews also moved to Essex, Northamptonshire and Kent where they settled in Lewisham.
During the eighteenth century more Morphews settled in the American colonies as 'Servants' working on the tobacco plantations.
In the nineteenth century Morphews moved across Britain. Morffews lived mainly in Surrey in the Ham and Kingston area but later moved to Chelsea.
The 19th century was a century of migration in England and across the sea.
In Norfolk Morphews are found in Costessey, Norwich and Great Ellingha, Later in the 1820s some moved to Great Yarmouth but towards the end of the century few Morphews could be found in Norfolk.
In Sussex most Morphews were living in Rotherfield and East Grinstead where prominent blast furnaces worked. But the industry died out and moved

north. In the 1820s Morphews were living in Horsted Keynes and later Lewes and Hastings.

The 19th century saw a number of Morphews move to Kent, by 1820 they were living in Gillingham.

As London developed more Morphews moved to Lewisham and Deptford in Southwark.

About 1850 several Morffews migrated to Australia settling at Melbourne and and then Ballarrat at the time of the gold rush.

Morphews moved to other counties, including Lincolnshire and Cornwall

In the late 1800s some Morphews moved to Canada and settled in the Ontario region. This patern carry on in to the 20th century.

In America Morphews settled and lived mainly on the Eastern Sea Board

Through out the 20th century and in to the 21st century Maufes, Morphews and Morffews are found living across the globe but predominently in the United Kingdom.

In the beginning.
Vikings; their Colonisation of Northern France

The Vikings (Norsemen) were seafarers who's influence spread far across Europe in to Byzantium, (modern day Turkey)
Vikings sailed down the long rivers that lead from Northern Europe to the Black Sea and served in the Varangian Guard, an elite unit in the Byzantium Army..
Vikings also raided across Northern Europe including France where they attacked Paris after sailing down the Seine.
In 911 the King of France ceded a parcel of land to Rollo, a Viking leader, under an agreement they would protect the mouth of the Seine and stop any other Viking raiders sailing along it.
These Vikings were originally from Denmark and many settled in this small pocket of land at the mouth of the Seine near Rouen.
Over time Vikings from Sweden, Norway and some of those who had earlier settled in England resettled in what was to become known as Normandy and Ireland.
The Norse language of the Vikings gradually died out as they adopted French. This is refered to as the 'Romance Language', derived from Latin. The French spoken by the Normans was a rural dialect known as Anglo Norman, or Norman French which is different to the French spoken in Paris of the time, this was known as Francien.
Normandy became too small for the growing population of Normans. They expanded their territory by invading adjacent land to the west taking territory from the Breton's.

Normandy eventually became a Duchy whose influence extended far beyond its borders.

Normans travelled to Southern Italy hiring them selves out to the highest bidder in the local wars. They gained land, wealth and an enviable reputation as they conquered Southern Italy and eventually Sicily.

Normans settled in Liberia (Catalonia, Spain) where they fought against the Moores as Crusaders.

The 7th Duke of Normandy, (William I) laid claim to the throne of England resulting in the Norman invasion of England in 1066.

This claim to the English throne came about when in 1002 Ehelred the Unready, the English King married Emma of Normandy, the sister to Richard II, Duke of Normandy. Their son Edward the Confessor spent time exiled in Normandy.

Edward invited Norman assistance to England. Norman courtiers, soldiers and clerics were appointed in to prominent positions.

The Normans supported Edward in his conflict with Godwin, Earl of Wessex and his sons. But Edward was eventually forced to expel the Normans from England after a rebellion.

When Edward the Confessor died childless there were several claims to the English throne, including one from William, Duke of Normandy. He claimed to have been promised the throne by Edward the Confessor but Harold Godwinson, Earl of Wessex became the next king of England.

1066. The Norman Invasion

In 1066 the 7th Duke of Normandy, 'William the Bastard' gathered a large fleet and army in Normandy for an invasion of England. Normandy supplied the bulk of the army and fleet but others joined ~~from~~ the enterprise from neighbouring dukedoms, domains and principalities including Brittany. Also some Normans ~~returned from~~ Southern Italy. *[had been settled in Italy fighting]*

Williams's large fleet landed on the Sussex coast at Pevensey Bay. At the time this was an estuary not the pebble beach it is today, on 28th September. On 14th October King Harold's army arrived at Hastings after a long ~~gruel~~ *arduous* march having defeated the Vikings at Stamford Bridge.

Harold's army held the high ground as Williams's army attacked up hill. Both sides fought hard with no quarter given from either side. Many were killed on both sides, including the Anglo Saxon King, Harold II. At one point it was thought William had been killed until he lifted his helmet to show he was still alive.

After Harold was killed the Anglo Saxon army waivered then fled with Norman cavalry in close pursuit hacking at them as they tried to escape. The battle at Hastings had lasted most of the day and only stopped at dusk. After the battle of Hastings William's army marched on London, crossing the River Thames at Wallingford. William was crowned King William I in Westminster Abbey on Christmas Day.

To secure his new Kingdom William gave land to Barons and Knights. A defensive line was established, stretching from the Wash in Norfolk to the River Severn in the west with Motte and Bailey castles constructed on hills through out the land.

was Meyhet Maffe from Southern Italy. Had a sister and looked like a muslim.

South of this defensive line land was taken from the Anglo Saxons, particularly in Sussex and Kent.
William used Sussex to quickly travel to the south coast when he needed to return to Normandy which he still ruled. Ensuring he had a safe passage Sussex was divided in to five, later six regions called Rapes. Each ran north to south across the county.

Each Rape was only entrusted to Williams most loyal Barons, most notably his relatives. These Rapes were Chichester, Arundel, Bramber, Lewes, Pevensey and Hastings.

William I built an Abbey at Battle, Sussex to commemorate his victory and in remembrance of those who helped him win the battle. A Roll was compiled by a monk and is known as the Battle Abbey Roll. Over time copies have been made but the original has been lost. Historians have tried to establish the authenticity of the names inscribed in the 17th century copies by Holinshed, Duchesnes and Leland.

The Holinshed lists Maufe, Duchesnese lists Mauley and the Leland roll lists 'Menyle et Maufe'. The Dive su Mere Roll in Normandy does not list any of these names. Alternative spelling has been put as Mengle which could be an entirpretation from the faded document. Today there are people living in Normandy whose family name is Mengle. It could be possible the Mengle or Menyle family lived in Maufee (Meauffe) at the time of the invasion.

The Hollingshed Roll listing those who arrived with William I, it has the name Manfe and Maule. Again this can be a miss-spelling from the faded document.

William encouraged Norman's to settle in England. He passed a law that gave Anglo Saxon land and property to a Norman when he married in to an Anglo Saxon family.

22

The Normans embarked on a castle; fort building project. These were motte and baily castles at first. They entailed a tall mound of earth with steep sides. The castle; fort was constructed of wood initially, that was quick and easy to build. Later they were fortified with stone walls.

William also built a tower in London on the River Thames. This tower was over seen by Gundulf, the Abbot of Bec in Normandy and became The Tower of London. He also built a new castle at Windsor close to the older Anglo Saxon castle.

The families of those who had died at Hastings were invited to cross the Channel and take up land thus rewarding their sacrifice. Those who supported the most with ships and soldiers were rewarded the most with land in England.

The Maufe family appear to take the opportunity and settled in Northamptonshire and Sussex.

William experienced a number of rebellions across the country by Anglo Saxons. The first one in 1067 made William return from Normandy and was put down. This was followed by more rebellions in 1069. One rebellion was in alliance with the Danes who raided along the East Coast. William paid the Danes to leave which they did. This left William to concentrate in subduing the Anglo Saxon rebels. He sent Earls to put down the rebellion in the south. In the winter of 1069-70 William took a large army partly composed of mercenaries north to 'Harry the north'. This was cruel and indiscriminate, people were killed, crops and dwellings burnt, animals slaughtered and farming tools destroyed. Sixteen years later the Yorkshire and Durham entry in the Domesday Book of 1086 says they were 'layed waste'.

Having subdued the rebellions William replaced all of the Anglo Saxon Lords with Normans and a loyal Breton in North Yorkshire.

During this time Franco Norman developed in to Anglo Norman which was the language of the Kings and nobility of England. The peasants and lower classes of England spoke Old English which the Normans considered to be vulgar. The two languages developed side by side over time with the introduction of new words from France and other European regions.

The day to day trades such as bakers, millers, shoe maker kept their Anglo Saxon titles whilst the skilled trades such as masons, painters, taylors, merchants, etc adopted Anglo Norman titles.

Give examples of Anglo Norman spellings

11th Century

The earliest record we have of Maufé (Malfet) settling in England is in 1078; a William Malfet gave half hide (about fifteen acres) of land at Possingworth, Sussex to the church or priory of St. Pancras in Lewes, Sussex. Possingworth is in the Weald of Sussex and Surrey. An 1898 map shows Possingworth surrounded by arable fields interspersed with woodland, the land is relatively flat. In 1078 the woodland would have been more extensive prior to the trees being felled for the Royal Navy and making charcoal in the 15th, 16th and 17th centuries. The Weald of Sussex and Surrey is a wide geological enscarpment in Southern England. This chalk enscarpment is known as the North and South Downes. At the time of the Norman invasion there were just a few small communities.

About 1086 William Malfeld, son of William Malfeld gave "terram de Ruecningiis" with its marshes, and Terra de Nathewerda, (Netherfield)" and five solidutes of land in Nordhorseya, (Horse Eye, Sussex). Horse Eye is a large area of natural beauty called the Horse Eye Level, with open fields and marshes. Drainage ditches criss cross the level. A Solidute was relaimed land, in this case marshland drained ready for planting. It has most probably not changed much since 1086. Horse Eye is east of Hailsham, a medium size town. Virtually in the middle of this open countryside is a manor called Horse Eye.

In 1086 William conducted a survey of England's assets. The survey became known as the Domesday Book. This was to record who owned what land, how much they owned, their dwelling, their property and how many vassals (individuals owing homage) lived and worked on the land. One entry mentions the Maufé

25

family in Northamptonshire at Woodford in the Hundred of Huxlow. First knight enfeoffed (given land in return of pledged loyalty) by the Abbey to Woodford. Woodford is about twenty five miles north east of Northampton. Woodford is a village on a bend in the River Nene and surrounded by flat arable land and woodland.
Woodford is on the west of the river Nene where the land rises. On the east of the river the flat fields tend to flood.
This holding included 7 hides (land, 7 Hides equates to about 840 acres), land for 12 ploughs. In demesne there were 2½ ploughs and 4 serfs. There was a mill attached to the manor, (Woodford Lenton Manor), giving 2 shillings and 20 acres of meadow. It was worth 20 shillings but by the time of the Domesday recording was 60 shillings'. Because the village Mauffe in Normandy is by the river, La Vire the Malfed/Maufe family might have had experience of running a water mill.
The advowson, (the right to select the priest) in Woodford was held by Maufé.
The Domesday Book records Rogerius Malfed (Roger Maufé) held land for Peterborough Abbey.
A Guy Maufé in the same survey held land in Hemington, a small village north east of Woodford. Hemington is on high ground that slopes gently away, this gives a good view when looking north. There is some woodland near bye but it is mostly arable fields. A map dated 1836 looks very similar to what it is today. Pytchleys book of fees mentions '2 knights fees which includes Kingsthorpe, both held for Peterborough Abbey. One of the fee's for Maufe also included land in Woodford and Hemington. Kingsthorpe was written as Chingestorp, Kyngesthorp and Kynestorp.
Looking at a map of Northamptonshire today the village

of Woodford is about ten miles from the village of Hemington. There is a manor at Hemington and several cottages. Less than one mile from Hemington is Kingsthorpe Lodge and Kingsthorpe Coppice. Linked with the land of Kingsthorpe is the hamlet of Armston which was part of the land owned by Guy Maufé, who held a hide of land for the Abbey. Part of his fee seems to have been included in Hervey de Borham's grant to Thorney Abbey, of the manor of Kingsthorpe and was still held in 1291. The Domesday book records an estimated nine households, nine villagers, six freemen and three small holders. The lord had five men at arms which included those in Armston.

Information dating from 1381 describes the topography of Kingsthorpe as fields but mentioned little of the village.

Three charters dated about this time mention a Simon Maufe.

The Domesday Book also records a Guy Maufe holding a $5/8^{th}$ of a hide (about 75 acres).

William I died in1087 whilst fighting against the French. William the Conquer was succeeded by his son William II, the third son of William I, also known as William Rufus.

In 1096 a Pierre de la Meauffe took the cross as an English Crusader and embarked on the First Crusade to the Levant. His coat of arms was 'Vert (Green) 3 fleur-de-lis or'.

This family name spelling is interesting, The book 'English Crusaders' written by Dansey James Cruikshank in 1850 gives the same spelling as the contemporary name for the village in Normandy.

Many who embarked on the First Crusade died enroute through starvation, thirst or in battle. When the Crusaders captured Jerusalem many settled and made

it their home.
There is no record of Pierre de la Meauffe returning.

12th century

1100 William Rufus died whilst hunting, he was shot by an arrow. William was succeeded by Henry I.

About 1100 a William Maufe married Basile Denny at Buckhurst in Sussex. Buckhurst was owned by Ralph Dene. There is no record of Basile Denny being related to the Dene family.

In Northamptonshire during 1112, Guy Maufe, a knight of Benceline de la Mare recieved her permission to grant his tithes, (taxes) to the church.

An Inquisition In 1114 states 'in Hemington during the reign of Henry I, Guy Maufe, second of three knights, possible heir of Roger Malfet or Malfed tenant of Woodford and son of Guy Maufe, wife Adeliza', granted land to the abbey and was confirmed by Henry I. Guy Maufe was still in possession of land in 1117.

Also mentioned in records is a Roger Maufe In the 1125 – 1128 Rolls reduced the holding to 5 hides, (a Hide was about 120 acres) and 3 virgates, (a virgate was equivalent ot about 30 acres), together with the soke (a Anglo Saxon and Norman legal term) of 3 hides of land of which Gislebert, son of Richard, was the tenant.

The Northamptonshire lands in Woodford and Kingsthorpe and probably Hemington were held by the service of two knights' fees and castle guard at Rockingham.

Rockingham is 2 miles north of Corby, Northamptonshire. William I ordered a Motte and Bailey castle to be constructed at Rockingham, William II replaced it with a stone castle. A stone keep was added to the large Motte and outer Bailey was enclosed by a curtain wall.

The castle was used as a royal retreat by the Normans and Plantagenet kings where they hunted deer and wild boar. In 1270 Henry III strengthened the castle. Edward III was the last monarch to visit the castle. During 1130 there are two entries in the Pipe Rolls (financial records) from Northamptonshire relating to Maufe.
One is for Guy Maufe, "renders account of one war-horse that he may be justly treated in court of his lord. In the treasury 40 shillings in place of one war-horse".
A War Horse was specially trained and ready for a knight to use in battle or tournaments. It was more expensive than other horses of the time and highly prized by knights. They were agile and had strong hind quarters. They were smaller than a draught horse such as a Shire.
The 40 shillings fee might also have included the reins and saddle, hence the high price.
Another entry in the Pipe Rolls is of a Wido Malfeth (Maufe).

Henry I died in 1135 at St. Denis et Lyons. Henry was succeeded by Stephen Blois.
Roger Maufe was succeeded by Guy Maufe who with his wife Adeliza gave portion of his tithes to Peterborough in 1141, the year when King Stephen fought at the Battle of Lincoln and was captured.
Guy Maufe gave the Peterborough Abbey tithes which he had been with holding, this was half a hide and half a virgate. He was succeeded by Simon Maufe, possibly his son.
During 1147 in Northamptonshire Alexander Maufe issued a foundation (privileges) charter to Sawtry

Abbey on behalf of Simon II of Senlis, Earl of Northampton and Huntingdon. The Earl of Northampton claimed more land that was endowed to the manor of Sawtry Judith. The Jurors swore the boundaries were of the manor since the time of Turchil the Dane.

Simon II fought on the side of King Stephen during the rebellion. Simon II married the daughter of the 2nd Earl of Leicester. Alexander Maufe was a tenent of Simon II of Senlis in Huntingdonshire. About the same time there is a record of Alexander Maufe on the moiety (divided in parts) of the Church at Heminctone (Heminstone, Suffolk). A record of Simon (son of Alexander Malfe) having the moiety of Heminctone Church.

On the document for the moiety there is a green wax seal three inches in diameter. It bares a male griffin surrounded by the text "SIGILLUM SIMONIS... ....MALFE". There is the same seal on a record for Messuage (dwelling with out buildings and land associated) in Hemictone.

This document high lights how two entries of the same family can have two different spellings. Hemingstone is a small village situated on a road junction between Ipswich, Bury St Edmunds and Colchester, mid Suffolk. The surrounding country side is typically flat for this part of England divided into fields with woods to the east.

Stephen Blois died at Dover in 1154 and was succeeded by Henry II.

1165 William Malfed was enfeoffed to supply three knights to Richer de Aquila in Sussex.

1166 William Malfeth/Malfed/Maffay is mentioned in the Lewes Chartulary (Sussex), "William son of William Malfed gave "ecclesiam de Hekintona cum duabis vigatis terre", (the church of Hekington, Lincolnshire with duabis vigatis land).

Richard Baron d'Aquila grants gifts to the church, also to William Malfet "namely half a hide Posingewrda (Possingworth, Sussex) and five shillings worth of land at Lamberst, (Lamberhurst, Kent)". Of the witness signatories is a William Maufey in the same document, it looks as though the witness was the beneficiary, but spelt differently.

In 1166 William Malfed held three knights fees of the Count of Eu at Hechestone (Eckington) and Ripe.

The Count of Eu and Lord Hastings was John, Henry I son.

1176 the Cambridgeshire Rolls states 'Guy Maufe succeeded by Simon le Malfe with Alexander Maufé having some right to advowson and holding land at Hemington

1179 at Woodford, Northamptonshire there is a mention of a Simon Maufe holding the two knights fees and also later in 1189.

In 1180 Robert de Grafham recovered the right to half knights fee in Wooley from Simon de Maufe.

1181 Simon Maufé was a tenant of Wooley, Huntingdonshire, (Cambridgeshire).

1187 Maufe family is recorded holding the Manor of Wooley, Huntingdonshire. The tenenant is Simon Maufe.

Wooley is about 15 miles south of Peterborough, 20 miles south east of Hemington and some 15miles east of Woodford

Henry II died 1189 at Chinon, France. He was succeeded by Richard I, 'Richard the Lion Heart'.

Simon Maufe is mentioned holding two fees in 1189.

Extract from the the Calendar of Charters relating to the Abbey of Robertsbridge, Sussex says the following. "Grant fee of land which was Robert Truths which he held of Adam de Cobbeford. And which the said Adam gave in marriage with Hodierna his sister to the grantor. Subject to the yearly rent of 2 shillings and 6 pennies and of free service due to the King and the Lords of the soil. This agreement was made with the consent of William Maufe capital Lord of the fee consolidation money one mark". One of the witness's was William Maufe.

Another entry from the same Calendar Charter records interestingly Philip Malfe, Milis Maufe, Philip Maufai and Milo Maufye. Showing that the Maufe name can be inconsistantly spelt several times in the same document.

1191 John Malfey is at Kings Lynn

1196 Lucas Maufe succeeding Simon Maufe. He is mentioned in Northamptonshire Curia Regis Rolls 1196-1202, at Kings Lynn. Holding land in Woodford Manor, Northamptonshire. Having died this was given to his younger son.

In 1194 there is a manuscript in Latin recording a Hugo Maufe and others giving alms.

1198 in Norfolk Simon Malfei in Feet of Fines.

Richard I died in 1199 at Châlus, France. Richard was succeeded by John Lackland, 'King John'.

13th Century

1203 Roger Malfe in Northamptonshire is mentioned in Rotulus Cancellarii

1205 Lucas Maufe at Woodford, Northamptonshire enters in to an agreement of advowsant, (right to select the priest), with Walter Tailly.

1210-1212 Simon Maufé held half knights fee in Wooley, Huntingdonshire in honour of Duke of Gloucester.

Extracts dated about 1210 - 1215 from Calendar of Charters and documents relating to to the Abbey of Robertsbridge. The dates were not written in the book, but it mentions a Milo Maufye, Maufie and Maufe.

"Milo, (Miles) Maufye to Gervase son of Andrew de Winchelese. Grant for 24 marks of all the land he once held of Adam de Cobeford in Walderne. To hold freely of the said Adam and his heirs subject to the yearly render to himself and his heirs of one pound of wax for all service save that due to the said Adam. — Witnesses; William de Muncell, Henry de Prestun, Thomas de Burthune, Herebert de Burgherse, Richard de Gare, Rennger de Bosco, Henry de Berch:, William de Sokenesse, Symon de Hydenye, Alan of Robertsbridge, Thomas de Harmere, Thomas de Holt, William his son".

"Confirmation of all the land which was once Milo Maufie's, being of his fee and which Gervase son of Andrew de Winchelese gave them in frank-almoign (in English law, a religious holding of land given to them), and in respect of which they rendered him (Adam) 12d yearly at their grange called Derne; quit of [sic] all service save the King's scutage as much as

belongs to a twentieth part of a knight's fee. —
Witnesses : Henry de Prestune, Robert de Glotingeham, Adam his son, Henry de Birche, Alan of Robertsbridge, Richard Venator, Ralph de Feme, Alan his brother, Thomas de Houte, William his son, Walter Folet, Gilbert his brother".

Yet another record says the following.

"Sale, for loss. And a seam of corn, of a yearly rent of 12d. which they were wont to pay him in respect of a tenement they held of him in Slohtre, so that neither he nor his heirs will make any claim either upon Slohtre or the land which was Milo Maufe's. — Witnesses: Thomas de Burton, Robert de Manekes, Thomas de Bestonore, Simon dc Ydeney, Henry de Berche, Richard de Camera, William irisilun, Thomas de Holt, William his son, John Frankeleyn, William Royfer, Symon de Grave".

"Sale, for a seam of corn, of a yearly rent of 2d., part of a rent of year., they were wont to jxiy [sic] him in respect of a tenement
they held of him in Slohtre, so that in future neither he nor his heirs will make any claim either upon Slohtre or the land which was Milo Maufye's, save the King's scutage on the latter, except for 2s a year _ Witnesses : Robert de Glottingeham, Adam his son, Henry".

"Grant, in frankalmoign, of all the land of Eylbrihtesham, (Sussex) which Adam his father gave him for his free service, and lying between the land which was once Mylo Maufye's, towards the south, and the
land which Geoffrey the grantor's brother holds of the Lord of Ronde, and the land of his brother Robert

towards the west, and the gate".

"Confirmation of all the lands and tenements given them by Adam his father. All the land of Slohtre lying between the water which runs from Slohtre Bridge and the King's Highway leading from the said bridge to Walderne (Waldron) Forest and the land which was Milo Maufe's. Also all the land given them by Gervase Andrews of Winchelese, who bought it of Milo Maufe, and all the land of Eylbrihtesham together with that part of it and the grove".

Reading through these records in the Calendar of Charters for the Abbey of Robertsbridge in Sussex we see that Milo (Miles) has his name spelt several ways. Mailfe, Maufey, Maufe, Maufie and Maufye

1211-12 there is a mention of a William Maufe at Woodford Northamptonshire.

1216 King John died at Newark on Trent. He was succeeded by Henry III.

1219, Walrand Maufe was a witness to a charter for the donation of land by Gilbert de l'Aigle. The same year William de Beauchamp gave the king 5 marks for summoning Oliver Maufe before the itinerant justices in Huntingdonshire to pay him 35 marks. He had a writ ordering the sheriff of Huntingdonshire to take security from William for those 5 marks for the king's use from the first monies. Witness; the Bishop of Winchester.

1221 Thomas Morphe/Maufe/Maufle mentioned in a Piper Rolls, (county unknown).

Record of William Maufe dying before 1224 in Woodford, Northamptonshire. He was succeeded by Robert Maufe who held the two fees but granted the Abbot of Thorney certain lands in Kingsthorpe.

In 1225 an Order to the sheriff of Sussex 'to take into the king's hand the land of William Maufe.

Waleran Maufe disseised (dishonestly sold) the same William by his own authority, and to keep it safely until the king orders otherwise'.

Oliverus (Oliver) Maufe is mentioned in the 1232 Close Rolls.
An entry in the Patent Rolls 1232-1247 'acknowledge of the receipt in the wardrobe at Hereford on Tuesday the eve of St. Andrew Henry III by the hand of P. de Rivollis 17 shillings and Oliver Maufe collects of the 40th 17 shillings and 10 pennies in Huntingdonshire delivered to him
1233 Close Rolls states William Maufe as a witness requesting the King, Henry III to come before the benches relating to land holdings.
In 1235 Walram Maufe is mentioned in a patent roll relating to arrest and gaoling.
"the like of Walram, Godfrey le Wales, Laurence de Mundefeld and Amfrey de Fering as justices to deliver the gaol of E. Archbishop of Canterbury of Otteford in Kent at Lewes, on Monday after mid-lent of Hawise de Maggefeld. Detained there for false charge and mandate to the archbishop bailiff of Otteford to have her before them".

Between 1241 and 1269 Malram Maufe is enfeoffed to supply three knights to Peter de Savoy.
Peter de Savoy was a Count of Savoy. He came to England in 1240 at the invite of Henry III. Eleanor of Provence, Henry III Queen was Peter de Savoy's niece.

Eleanor brought a number of her relatives to England who were also given lands and manors held by other nobles.

Peter de Savoy was given the honour of Richmond, Yorkshire in 1240. He was also given land in London and built Savoy Palace. This was later owned by John of Gaunt and burnt down during the Jack Cade Rebellion of 1450.

Peter also obtained the manor of Boston in Lincolnshire and possibly manor of Donington in Derbyshire. In 1246 Henry III granted Peter de Savoy Pevensey Castle in Sussex. He became Sheriff of Kent and granted Rochester and Dover Castles. He was also given Wardenship of the Cinque Ports, (several ports along the Sussex and Kent coast that held special trading priverleges. Today this is an honoury title.

In 1241 Henry III sent Peter de Savoy to France too gather support for an invasion of Poitou, West France. He met with Hugh IV, Duke of Burgundy; Theobald of Navarre, Amadeus IV Count of Savoy and Ramon Berenguer IV Count of Provence. He then went to Poitou to see what support there might be for Henry but was nearly captured by French soldiers.

In 1241 Alice Maufe gave 1 mark for having a pone (to remove a plea) from the county court of Essex to (the eyre of the justices) at Canterbury. 'Order to the sheriff of Essex'.

In 1242 Peter de Savoy sailed with Henry III and his army to Poitou. This expedition did not fare well and the invading army was defeated at the Battle of Taillebourg.

Peter de Savoy had to attend to trouble in Savoy and Henry supplied money and men.

In 1242 Oliver Maufe was tenant in Wooley,

Woolley

Huntingdonshire. Today Wooley is a hamlet in Cambridgeshire. Wooley is written in the Domesday Book as Cileulai.

The Domesday Book records 14 households living there. The countryside around Wooley is open arable fields that gently undulates. Wooley is about two miles north of a river. To the east is an old moat. There are lodges and a manor in the surrounding area and remains of a castle to the west. Foundations of an old village are near the castle.

Oliver Maufe was succeeded by Simon Maufe who married Brunna, a daughter and co heir of Ralph de St. Sampson. The Samson family held land across England. This was awarded by William I after the invasion.

1242 in Close Rolls a fine was imposed on John Maufe, knight of Hunterdon, Sussex, '…..acknowledges he owes to Nicholas de la Beche, knight 300 shillings to be levied in default payment of his lands and chattels in the county of Sussex'.

About this time John de Maufe held a knights fee, (land) at Haselbury, Northamptonshire in the name of Roger de Quincy, 2nd Earl of Winchester. Born around 1195 and died in 1264. He held the title of the Constable of Scotland. At the time of his death he was one of the largest land holding barons in both England and Scotland.

During the Baron War Roger de Quincy opposed Henry III but died soon after the Civil War had started. The Earldom of Winchester died with Roger de Quincy but his extensive estates were divided between his three daughters.

Roger de Quincy was a prominent nobleman. He held land in England and Scotland. Much of the land was gained through his three marriages.

It would appear that Oliver and John Maufe might have been connected in some way with the Poitou invasion. There is only one mention of Malram Maufe and could have been obliged to accompany Peter de Savoy on the expedition.

Peter returned to England in 1247 and was given the honour and castles of Hastings and Tickhill in Yorkshire.

Peter was ambassador for Henry on a number of occasions in France and Scotland.

He was also a negotiator for Henry with the Barons and Simon de Monfort.

When the 2nd Baron war broke out Peter de Savoy left England because of the animosity towards all foreigners. Even so Peter retained his lands in England until his death in 1266.

Patent Rolls of 1247-1258 'King Henry III selling land to settle Kings Debts. Knight Simon Maufe to associate with Huntingdon commissioner'

24 Nov 1248 at Huntingdon, 'William de la Bruere and Simon Maufe. William de la Bruere, who has taken to wife Joan, first-born daughter and one of the heiresses of Ralph de St. Samson, and Simon Maufe, who has taken to wife Briminatyn, later-born daughter and the other heiress of the aforesaid Ralph, have performed their homage to the king for all lands and tenements that Ralph held of the king in chief. Order to Henry of Wingham and his co-escheator in Northamptonshire and Bedfordshire to cause William and Joan, Simon and Briminatyn to have full seisin without delay of all lands and tenements formerly of the same Ralph in the aforesaid county, of which Ralph was seised [sic] as of fee on the day he died and which fall to Joan and Briminatyn by inheritance, having accepted sufficient security from William and Joan, Simon and Briminatyn for rendering their reasonable relief to the king for this

at the king's summons'.

1248 Close Rolls 'Brunna, daughter of Ralph de St. Sampson and wife of Simon Maufe inherited Grafton Underwood Manor in Northamptonshire. This is about 5 miles to the west of Woodford, near Kettering'. Today Grafton Underwood Manor is refered to as a 16th century listed building. The surrounding countryside is flat open fields and woodland to the north.
Grafton Underwood Manor was given in part to his two daughters and by joint agreement sold the manor to Elizabeth Neville.
Also in 1248 Close Rolls 'King looking Maufe Simon gave himself a soldier of the performing up to Easter and a command is ordered Huntingdon'.
Also 'Simon Maufe functions in terms of the soldiers performing up to Christmas the year. The command is ordered Huntingdon etc'.
1251 in Northamptonshire. 'John Clerk and William Maufe gave the king one mark for taking an assize before G. of Preston. Order to the sheriff of Northamptonshire to take security'.
In 1252 Northamptonshire. 'William Maufe gave the king one mark for having the writ quare vi et armis [returnable] before the king (coram Rege). Order to the sheriff of Northamptonshire........'
In 1253 Northamptonshire. 'William Maufe de Heychinton' gives the king one mark for having a pone [to remove a plea] before the justices at Westminster. Order to the sheriff of Northamptonshire to take etc'.
Robert Maufe of Woodford, Northamptonshire died in 1254, he left four daughters as his heirs. The fee, (land) was divided between them. The eldest daughter married Thomas Deyville. The second daughter, Alice

married John de Bois. Joan the third daughter married but no name recorded. The fourth daughter married Roger de Kirkton.
Joan had two daughters. When Joan died the Woodford manor was divided between them.

The records of the manorial administration of Kingsthorpe Northamptonshire entered in the Pytchley's Book of Fees mentions two fees, which included Kingsthorpe land, both held of Peterborough Abbey. One of these, the fee of Maufe, also included land in Woodford and Hemington and was rated at 2 knight's fees.
Before 1254 Robert de Vere granted tenements of this fee in Hemington and Kingsthorpe to the abbot of Thorney.
1254 Maufe in Northamptonshire mentioned as a witness.
1255 Simon Maufe is mentioned in Calendar of patent rolls along with Walter de Wassingle at Huntingdon.
1256, concerning fines of gold. 'Simon Maufe of Huntingdonshire gave the king half a mark of gold for the same which he paid in the king's Wardrobe to Artald de Sancto Romano and is quit'.
In the same year Simon Maufe was mentioned in a patent roll relating to individuals being excused assizes, juries or recognitions, from being a sheriff, escheator, verderer, forester, agister, or bailiff for the King.

1260 record, 'Sire Waleron Maufe, Alice Maufe and Sir William Maufe mentioned in deeds and documents relating to wedding gifts in Battle, Sussex. "her land of pelings (in Westham, Sussex) with the homages, rents, suits of court and other appurtenances which her father

Sir Waleran Maufe gave her in free marriage. An annual rent of 5 shillings which Walter de Bosco was accustomed to pay which she has by the gift of her

mother Alice Maufe. Witnesses: Sir William Maufe, Sir Jordan de Saukewile, William de Bestenovere, Berenger Tirel, the brothers Gervase and Robert de Bestenovere, Richard le Brade, Simon de Hellingelee, Lawrence de Horsie, Richard and Hugh de Camera, Alexander de Rattone".
This document shows us that the Maufe have come of some standing with two Maufe refered to as Sir in a document.
Amongst the witness's is an interesting person, Sir Jordan de Saukewile (Sackville) who's family was to own extensive lands in Sussex, Surrey and Suffolk.
In 1262 the Feet of Fines records a Henry de Morf, " A Messuage and half virgate of land and a fourth of Virgate in Prenestorp and Stratton-upon-Dunnesmore, Warwichshire. William Chacero and his heirs to hold tenement of Henry and Isabella, his wife and heirs of Isabella for a farthing annually".
Another entry at the year "Richard Walerand to hold messuage and virgate of land in Pernesthorp, Warwickshire. Richard and his heirs to hold tenement of Henry and Isabella for
12d yearly. Richard gave 20 marks".
Henry de Morf was a Verderer (forest warden) at Morf Forest in Staffordshire.

A further record of Henry de Morf mentions him as a Agistar. Agistars assisted the Verderers, (forest wardens). They managed the commoners free roaming animals grazing and charged a fee.
1263, 'William Maufe gives one mark for having an

attaint before the justices at the first session etc. Order to the Sheriff of Sussex. William Maufe gives half a mark for taking an assize before William of Wilton. Order to the Sheriff of Sussex'.

In 1264 the second Baron war involving the monarch Henry III and his son Prince Edward against Simon de Monforts army. This came to a head at the Battle of Lewes where the Barons were victorious Henry was forced to sign the Mise of Lewes. To ensure Henry kept to this treaty Prince Edward was held hostage. At some stage Edward managed to escape. This allowed Henry to rally his army and fought Simon de Monfort and his army at the Battle of Evesham where Simon de Monfort was killed.

William Maufe was paid a fee of 5 pennies at this time for guarding, possibly Lewes Castle.

The same year Henry III issued a letter of safe conduct, "safe conduct until Monday after the Feast of the Translation of St. Thomas the Martyr and for the whole of the day for Hanekin de Witsand, constable of Pevense Castle, John de le Rede and Imbert de Montreal. Summoned to come under the conduct of William Maufee whom the King is sending to bring them to speak to the king. As the King understands that many enormities have been committed by them and others of the munition of the castle".

We can surmise from this letter of safe conduct that those being summoned had possibly assisted Simon de Monfort. It also shows the amount of responsibility that was bestowed on William Maufee (Maufé).

1268 an interesting pardon is given by the King. "remission at the instance of John de Warrenna, Earl of Surrey to William Maufee of the Kings indignation and rancour of mind conceived towards him by occasions of

the trespasses which he said to have done at the time of the disturbance had in the realm and pardon to him of said trespasses.
John de Warrenna, (Warenne), 6th Earl of Surrey married Henry III half sister, Alice de Lusignan, an

extremely influencial family through out Europe at the time. John de Warrenne changed sides twice during the Baron Wars. He fled England when Henry was defeated at Lewes. Edward I made John de Warrenne Keeper of the Realm of Scotland but William Wallace defeated him at Stirling Bridge. He later accompanied Edward I on his Scottish campaigns. It could be possible the pardon was issued for going over to Simon de Monfort and for 'any trespass'. What ever the reason for the pardon, it became a long dispute between the Earl and William Maufee.

The Fine Rolls of 1270 to 1271 has an entry of a Henry de Morf (Morfe). He was a verderer (a warden of a Royal Forest) of Morfe Royal Forest in Staffordshire. Henry de Morfe, assisted with the prosecution of Richard de la Boruwe had taken a stag. Henry de Morfe held this title for a number of years and the land in the name of William de Burmingham. During the reign of Edward III Henry's son, John was his heir.
1270 'Robert Maufé gave a fee to the Abbot of Thorney'. That year it was recorded William Maufé held land in Hemington of two (knights), fees.
1271 In Pitsford, Northamptonshire Richard de Hanrede held the manor for William Maufe of Sussex. One of the mesne, (intermediate or intervening) lords who held it for Philip de Nevill.
Pitsford is a village surrounded by flat arable countryside. Today there is a reservoir to the north but

it is not shown on a map dated 1901. The River nene flows close by to the west.

In 1271 and 1272 Prince Edward attended a Crusade. This crusade was organised by Louis IX of France, a devout crusader. The crusade was intending to go to Egypt but Louis sailed to Tunis where Edward arrived later. Louis IX died in Tunis and many French Crusaders returned to France.

Edward decided to sail to the Levant (Holy Land) with his small force of 225 Knights and about 1000 foot soldiers.

This small army arrived at Acre and helped with the relief of the city. This army was later joined by an army from England and Cyprus lead by Edwards younger Brother, Edmund. This larger army supported by the Knights Templars, Hospitallars and Teutonic Knights carried out raids. The Crusade was not very successful and Edward returned home.

It would appear that William Maufe was with Edward on his Crusade. Having been awarded a heraldric arms possibly linked to the Crusade.

1272 Henry III died at Westminster Palace and was succeeded by Edward I

1272 William Maufe is mentioned in Sussex, deeds and documents held by the Fuller family.

From the inquisitions of Edward I, "That Jordan de Sakvill held a parcel of the manor of Chalvyngton (Chalvington) of William Maufe for castle guard 10 pennies and for Sheriffs aid 5 pennies as is contained in the extent therof after the death of the said Jordan". This William Maufe was owner Ekyngton (Ekington) which is now Gages. By Jordan de Sakewyle (Sackville), son and heir of Jordan de Sakewyl (Sackville) to Simon atte Wyseke, son of John le Haye of Burne of all that land with buildings and appurts, which Robert Wachard sometime held in the parish of Chalvyngton (Chalvington) lying in breadth between the way leading from Chalvyngton towards the Dyker (Sussex) and land of Lord William Maufe and extending in length from Dyker on the north to lands of Richard Wachard S."

This document shows us several things. A Maufe has become a Lord and he owns a manor, Ekyngton which changed its name to Gages was a Manor. Today a manor is still at Ekington on Church Lane between Ripe and Chalvington. This is a 18th century building, not the original. Ripe, Eckington and Chalvington are all mentioned in the Domesday Book. They date back to the Roman times who built a road through them. Chalvington was written Calvintone or Caveltone. Chalvington is a small village. Eckington written as Echentone in the Domesday Book, it sits on a cross roads not far is the village of Ripe. In medieval times the area had a profitable wool trade. Chalvington, Eckington and

Ripe are surrounded by flat open fields with very little woodland.

We see Jordan Sackville mentioned again three times in the document and also his son and heir. Each spelling is different which shows how the Maufe could easily be misspelt in the old documents.

1272 in Suffolk there is mention of Geoffry and Simon Malfey in the Rotuli Hundredorum.

1273 June 6th in Calendar of patent rolls in the time of Edward I.

A further announcement was issued, 'Mandaté to all persons in the counties of Surrey and Sussex to assist the sheriff in the preservation of peace'.

The main event of 1273 was Henry III had died in 1272 whilst Prince Edward was still abroad returning from his crusade. England was without a King and France might have had designs on invading or a possible rebellion by the barons. This mandate would have been a call for the Maufe family amongst others in these counties.

From a 1274 record, 'Gone beyond the sea's', a reference to going on a Pilgrimage or Crusade. 'Grant to William Maufe of the custody, during the minority of the heir of the following manors of late Jordon de Saukeville tenent in chief to wit the manor Sochurst extended twenty shillings in the Manor Chalventon, (Chalvington, Sussex), extended to sixty seven shillings four and three quarter pennies'. As appears in the inquisition made by Master Richard de Clifford'
This record instructs William Maufe to over see the late Jordon de Saukeville (Sackville) manors until his heir becomes of age.
1275 William Maufe mentioned in Sussex documents. In 1276 William de Maufe asked John de Alfriston for a messuage (accommodation) and land in Alfriston. Alfriston is a village in Sussex, in the Domesday Book it is written as Alvricestone. In a French document it is written as Alfrichestuna. There does not seem to be a record of William de Maufe receiving the messuage or land. It is also a mystery why he would have asked for it in Alfriston, except it is on the Cuckmere River.

1278 Sussex Fines Rolls ordered William Maufe to pay Mathew de Herne for the use of James, son of his brother, John de Herne ten marks from the Ferme of the town of Winchelse due from him on Michaelmas. William Maufe precided over sentencing in Surrey and

was recorded in the Surrey justices of Gaol delivery. He recorded the following sentencing.
1279 of 2 sentences, 1280 of 2 sentences, 1281 there were 4 sentences and 1282 only 1 sentence. This was very modest compared to others who precided over sentencing at the same time.

Between 1270 and 1280 the Dering Roll is compiled. The Dering Rolls are illustrated heraldic arms of 324 knights in several rolls. One of the Heraldic Arms is named as William Maufe or Malfe. The sheild is a standing black lion surrounded by eight red scallops on a white background (Argent Semée of Scallops gules, Lion Rampant, Sable). The written description says nine escallops but only eight are shown in the image on the derring roll.
The Lion signifies bravery and the scallop's pilgrimage To lands over sea's..
William Maufe Heraldic Arms is also in the Camden Rolls and a third Heraldic Roll dated later. Camden Rolls contains Heraldic Arms Emperors, Kings, English Earls, Sire Aunfour (Alonso of England, Earl of Chester, Eldest son of Edward I), Prince Gales (Prince of Wales), foreign counts, English Lords and Knights. During the reign of Edward I an Inquisition post Mortem records "Henry de Morf held quarter knights fee in honour of William de Burmingham at Evenfeld in Shropshire..
Another record during the reign of Edward I mentions Thomas de Morf who held Odecumbe, Somerset, by service"
In the 1275 Close Rolls (a Close Rolls was an administrative record to preserve a central record of all letters close by the chancery in the name of the Crown). 'to Guncelin de Badelesmere, justice of Chester to permit William Maufe and Joan his wife

relict of Thomas de Ippegrave to receive the toll that Thomas previously had at Chester of the Kings gift as the king granted to Joan by letters patent the said toll for her life in same way as Thomas held'.
1278 Edward I granted to William Maufee and Joan his wife 15 marks a year out of the ferm of the town of Winchelsea for the support of said Joan for her considering her surrender of the Gate of Chester which the King had given support.

1283 Close Rolls 'William Maufe held 2 fees in Westden and Bechinton, Sussex worth £10.
1285 William Maufe was a witness to a document for land and messuege being given to Peter Southgate and Jean his wife. This was in Bestenore and Horse Eyes (Horsye) in the Parish of Pevensey, Sussex.
1284 Henry Maufe born in Sussex married Joan de la Haye in Northamptonshire.
1285 William Maufe sat in Surrey Justices
1285 Simon Maufe in Northamptonshire
1285 Joan Maufe Northamptonshire.
From the Calendar Patent Rolls 1287, "commission with William Maufe and Luke late Gate re marsh landing
Megham. William Maufe obtained certain privileges for his tenants at Megham.
1288 William Maufe Surrey Justices

In 1290 at Winchelsea, Sussex there was a petition for Joan, late the wife of Thomas de Ippegrave, states that the king has granted her for life ten pounds a year from the town of Winchelsea, but the bailiffs claimed that the town is badly destroyed by the sea, make payment so

poorly that the ten pounds do not amount to as much as ten marks per year to her benefit.
'Therefore William Maufe and the said Joan, now his wife, request that they may hold the town for their Life time on payment of the farm to the king, and that the ten pounds a year may be allowed to them'.
Thomas d'Ippegrave was an English official who served under Henry III and Edward I. Thomas was

Member of the Privy Council, Constable of the Tower, Lord Mayor of London in 1268 and served as Senschal of Gascony from 1268 to 1269. Thomas was granted position of Serjent of Eastgate in the City of Chester of toll.
Thomas d'Ippegrave widow was granted the custody and tolls of the gate in 1278 which she surrendered to the crown in return for a pension.

1292 William Maufe mentioned in the Surrey Justices Sussex subsidy for 1292, in the Hundred de Wylyndon (Willingdon) in Rape of Pevense. The earliest subsidy for Sussex. Willo Maufe £3 2s 9¾d; Rogo Maufe 6s ¾d.
Hundred de Langebregg (Langridge) Rogero Maufe 9s 1d.
Villat de Hodlegh and Chytynelegh (Village Hoathley and Chiddingly) William Maufe 17s 11d.
Hoathley today is called East Hoathley. There is also West Hoathley in Sussex. The surrounding countryside is arable fields and woodland. In the 13th century there would have been substantially more woods. In the 16th century a lot of the woodland was felled for the Royal navy ships and charcoal for the blast furnaces and smelting iron. Chiddingly was occupied in Roman times

when sandstone was mined and iron ore extracted and smelted. Chiddingly is recorded in the Domesday Book as Cetelingei.
In the Middle Ages iron ore was smelted to make nails and other small iron work.
Patent Rolls of 1292 – 1301; 'Stepney commission de wallis et fossatis to Robert de Setvans and William Maufe in the county of Kent in the room of Henry de Apeltrefeud who is now by the kings command serving office of Sheriff in that county and Bertram Tann(cre) since deceased.
The 'commission de wallis et fossatis was a commission by the crown to supervise the sewers, drainage and flood protection.

The same Patent Rolls mentions Robert de Setvans, William de Hastings and William Maufe commissioned to supervise the sewers, drainage and flood protection in Kent and Sussex.
Association of William Colebraunt, Robert de Setvans, William de Hastings and William Maufe were commissioned to supervise the sewers, drainage and flood protection in Kent and Sussex.
Manuscript dated July 1293 mentions various knights fee's extended, "……In the said county (Sussex) which is extended at 40 shillings yearly, 1¾ that William Maufee holds in Chidyngele, Derne, Cobbeford and Alfritheston (Alfriston, Sussex). This is the first mention of the name Maufee in any documents.
1296, there are two entries in the Parliament Writs and Writs of Military Summons for William Maufe in Sussex. 'William Maufee, Williams Maufe enrolled pursuant to the ordinance for the defence of the sea coast as a knight holding lands within the Rape of Pevensey in Sussex'.

The next entry, 'William Maufe returned from counties of Sussex and Surrey as holding lands or rent to the amount of £20 yearly in person with horses and arms etc , in parts beyond the sea's . Muster at London on Sunday next after the Octaves of St. John the Baptist 7th July'.
In the 1296 Sussex Subsidy Roll for the Rape of Pevensey, (taxation records) there are four entries for Maufe.

Willo (William) Maufe for the sum of £3 2 shillings and 9¾ pennies.
Rogo (Roger) Maufe for the sum of 6 shillings and ¾ pennies. This is for Villat (village) Exete in the Hundred of Wylyndon (Willingdon), today refered to as Willingdon and Jevington.
Rogero (Roger) Maufe paid the sum of 9 shillings and one penny in the Hundred of Langebregg (Langbridge). Willingdon today is joined with Jevington. It is north of Eastbourne. In the Middle Ages Willingdon stretched across the north of Eastbourne reaching down to the English Channel. A 1890 map shows there are open fields around Willingdon, woods and copse are to the south. In the Middle Ages the woodland was more extensive.

Willimo (William) Maufe paid sum of 17 shillings and 11 pennies in the villat de Hodlegh (Hoathly) and villat Chytyngelegh (Chiddingly).
These records again show how names can be spelt differently in the same record when there is a Rogo and Rogero, the later is latinised. Also Willo and Willimo. Another entry in the Parliament Writs and Writs of Military Summons for 1297
'William Maufe summoned to appear with horses and

arms of a military council at Rochester before Edward the Kings Son and Lieutenant in England on Sunday nativity of the virgin 8th September'.

In these entries William is not referred to as 'Sir'. But he is expected to have horses and arms and be ready when reporting for military service.

January 1298 the King issues a grant in favour to William Maufee and his wife Joan. "To the Bailiffs of Winchelse (Winchelsea, Sussex) order to cause William Maufee and Joan, his wife, to have 100

shillings for Michaelmas term last from the ferm of the town, as the King granted to them by his letters of patent 15 marks yearly from the ferm by the hands of the bailiffs for Joan's maintenance, a moiety (to be divided) at Easter a moiety at Michaelmas and 100 shillings are in arrear for Michaelmas last".

14th Century

1300 document mentions Roggerus Maufe in a list of knights fee's in the Rape of Pevensey, Sussex.
1301–1307 Patent Rolls has two entries for William Maufe for Commissions de Wallis et fossatis.
The 1301 parliament Writs and Writs for Military Summons records William Maufe 'summoned from the Counties of Sussex and Surrey to perform military service in person against the Scots. To muster at Berwick on Tweed on Nativity of St. John the Baptist 24th June'.
Edward I assembled an army of 20,000 in Annan then relieve the garrison at Loch Maben castle. The English captured Caerlaveron after five days. The English then marched to Dumfries and Kirkcudbright and fought at Cree in August.
The English invaded Scotland again in 1303 and 1304.
September 1305 Sussex record 'John Hamund before the King sought to replvy (recover) to Roger Maufe later land in Estdene (East Dean). Taken into Kings Hands for his default before the justices ......'
John Hamund (Hammond) also tried to replevy (take back, recupe), to William Maufe his land in East Dene (East Dean) and West Dene, Sussex.
May 1306, "to the treasurer and barons of the exchequer. Order to all the baillifs of Wynchelese in their ferm 70 shillings for the twenty sixth to the thirtysecond year of the Kings reign inclusive, which they paid to William Maufee and Joan his wife a letter of patent accordance with the Kings order to pay them fifteen marks yearly which sum he granted to them. On 7th February in the sixth year of his reign. For the restitution that William and Joan made to him of the

custody of the Gate of Chester Castle which he had previously delivered to Joan for her maintenance. During 1306 and 1307 Edward I led an invasion of Scotland. On a subsequent attack on Scotland Edward died of dysentery at Burgh by Sands. Edward was succeeded by his son who was with his father on campaign. He stayed in the north but before long abandoned the campaign and returned south.

Entered in to various Rolls In the reign of Edward II (1307-1327) Andrew Maufe granted to the prior and convent of Mitchelham land in Folkington and Hailsham, Sussex.

During the reign of Edward II in the Plea of Rolls for Staffordshire Henry de Morf gave an oath in court of baring witness to a murder. Henry de Morf also bared witness with others at an inquisition that several individuals had broken into the castle of John de Somery at Duddeleye (Duddley) and stole £1000 or more.

1307 Andrew Maufe became rector of Fifield Bavant, Wiltshire. The rectorship was to last until 1317. He was licensed to study at an English University for five years during his incumbency. Fifield Bavant is a small village or hamlet, at the time the population was about 60, similar in size today. Fifield Bavant has a small church situated on a hill side. It is constructed of flint and stone.

Rectors were not obliged to stay within the parish. A rector might have the rectorship of several parishes. They could elect a vicar to stay in their absence, this could be a member of their family or close associate. The Rector would benefit from the tithes from each parish reaping a large quantity of corn.

Record for 1308. Five Peterborough tenants in Armston, Northamptonshire. One was Guy Maufé who held a Hide of land of the Abbey. There was a hospital at the prior of Armston. Armston is mile to the east of Kingsthorpe.

In1310 Edward II led an army in to Scotland.
During 1310 there are three records of Sire William Maufe receiving a payment of 5 pennies for guarding and another 'fee of ½ and ¼ held of William Maufe, rendering 10 pennies yearly for said guard'. William Maufe was also awarded a yearly fee of 2 shillings and 6 pennies for guarding Pevense Castle, Sussex. William Maufe now seemed to have acquired some standing and responsibility; he unlikely attended the 1310 invasion of Scotland but stayed in Sussex. This could have been in possible anticipation of a French Invasion whilst the King was in Scotland.

September 1311 'the Bailiffs of Winchelsea to pay Joan late the wife of William Maufe 15 marks yearly'. There is a similar record in 1313 for paying Joan 15 marks for the surrender of the custody of the Gate of Chester. This time the bailiffs refused to pay her.
1314 Maufé held half knights fee in honour of Gloucester at Wooley, Huntingdonshire.
The same year Edward II invaded Scotland with a large army of cavalry, Welsh archers and foot soldiers. The English encountered the Scottish Army lead by Robert the Bruce at Bannockburn. The battle started with the famous single combat of Robert the Bruce and Henry de Bohun. Upon Bruce winning the combat the Scottish army rushed at the English. The battle ensued with the Scots taking prisoners and forcing the English to retreat back to their original position.
During the night the English crossed a stream to gain

an advantage, at the same time a Scottish Knight with Edward deserted to Bruce and told him of the plan. Early the next morning the Scottish attacked the English taking them by surprise and hemmed them in making it difficult for the English Cavalry to manoeuvre and archers to fire who were charged by Scottish Cavalry.

Edward at this point was in danger and his house hold Knights lead him away to safety and he fled with a small force of Knights and Welsh Archers. The Scottish took no quarter in the battle, they were told not to take any prisoners during the battle. At the battles end a number of English had been taken prisoner, one of which was Thomas Maufe. [John]

The Scottish asked very high ransoms for the knights which many families found difficulty paying. The king refused to help pay any of the ransoms and many had to borrow the ransom money, in some cases from the church.

There is no mention of Thomas Maufe in later records leaving us to wonder if he was ever released or died in captivity.

There is a period when the Maufe's seem to owe money to various people. Maybe money was borrowed from these individuals to help release Thomas Maufe. He could have ended up in a monastery or having to work doing menial tasks.

In 1316 William Malfe or Maufee was certified as one of the Lords of the Townships of Ripe, Chiddlingley, Hoadley (Hoathly), Operton and Landport in Sussex. The Maufee spelling seems to be the first time it was used.

Today there is an East and West Hoathly in Sussex. West Hoathly was written as Hodlegh and East Hoathly was written as Hodleigh. Both villages are several miles apart.

In West Hoadly is a Chiddinglye Farm. Landport is an area of Lewes.

Close Rolls of 1316 mention 'John Maufe acknowledges that he owes to Nicholas de la Beche knight 300 shillings to be levied in default payment of his lands and chattels in Sussex.

In 1317 at Windsor the Close Rolls records Nicholas de Beche acknowledges that he owes to John de Maufe 100 marks to be levied in default of payment of his lands and chattels in Nottinghamshire.

John Maufe acknowledges that he owes to Nicholas de Beche 200 shillings to be levies in default of payment of his lands and chattels in Nottinghamshire.

John Maufe acknowledges that he owes to Nicholas de Beche 100 shillings to be levies in default of payment of his lands and chattels in Essex.

A complicated wrangle continuing from 1316 over debt between John Maufe and Sir Nicholas de la Beche who was seneschal of Gascony, a 14th century nobleman appointed constable of the Tower of London who died in 1345.

In 1318 and 1320 Henry de Morf was a witness to a deed relating to tenents of William de Perton.

Edward II attacked Scotland in 1319 and 1322.

Patent Rolls of 1321-1324 records 'license of alienation in mortmain to the Prior and convent of Michelham by Andrew Maufe of forty acres of land in Fokynton and ten acres in Hailsham.....'

In the Patent Rolls of 1324-1327 Andrew Maufe is mentioned. "license for the alienation in mortain to the prior and convent of Michelham by Andrew Maufe of 40 acres of land at Fokynton (Folkington, Sussex) and 10 acres in Hailesham, (Sussex). Not held in chief, as appears by inquisition made by William de Weston escheator in the counties of Kent, Sussex, Surrey and London. To hold as of the value of 40 shillings a year in part satisfaction of their license o acquire land and rent to the value of 20 marks a year.

In 1324 there was was an inquisition of post mortem in Sussex. "Joan late wife of William Maufee, Estbourne and Erlyngton 20 shillings yearly rent from John de Radmelde held of Lady Isabella, Queen of England. As of the honour of Laigle by fee and service of 1 penny for sheriffs aid yearly.

Chytynglegh, (Chittingly) twenty acres of land and 24 shillings and 3 pennies yearly rent held of Nicholas de Aldeham by service of 1/40 knights fee.

Claverham in Erlyngton 15 acres of land and 4 shillings 9 pennies rent, held of Sir John Ware by fee and service of 1 penny yearly. Andrew Maufee is her next heir". This appears to state who will inherit Joan's properties and rents and over see the services afforded to her in law. Possibly a last will and testament.

June 1324 William de Weston, escheator in Surrey, Sussex, Kent, Middlesex and the City of London. London was ordered "not to intermeddle further in the lands of Joan, late wife of William Maufee and to restore the issues there of as it appears by inquisition taken by the esheater that she held no lands of the King in Chief by reason where of the custody of her lands ought to pertain to the King".

We get an impression that Joan who was married to William Maufee (Maufé) had some sway but there is no obvious indication why.

Edward II died in 1327 at Berkley to be succeeded by Edward III.

At an inquisition during the reign of Edward III records a Thomas de Morf and heir of John de Morf. There is a descrepency over the rightful heir to property at Enefeld. "Wife of Thomas de Morf, Agnes fathers heir John de Morf".
1327 Calendar of the Patent Rolls records "The master Andrew Maufe, Laurence Maufe and others at Chidynlegh (Chittingly), Sussex broke his houses, felled his trees, mowed his meadow.

Thomas Maufee, Laurence Maufe (Maufei) and Andrew Maufe are mentioned in the Subsidy Rolls of 1327 – 1332 for Sussex. The subsidy rolls was a list of who were eligible to pay tax, the Poll Tax. This only applied to the males in well off house holds.
Villat de Brewyk (Berwick) Andrew Maufe 5 shillings 7¼ pennies; Villat de Westden (West Dene) and Excet Andrew Maufe 8 shillings and 11¼ pennies; Hundred de Estgrenstede (East Grinsted) Andrew Maufe 2 shillings and 6 pennies
We find Elias Maifai and William Mayfai are also mention in the 1327 subsidy rolls for Sussex.
East Grinstead was a Saxon hamlet. By 1086 it had grown to a large village. By the 13th century it was a town.
In 1247 East Grinstead was given a charter to hold weekly markets, and granted an annual fair. During the Middle Ages East Grinstead was a busy town, it was on the main road between Lewes and London and became a place to stop over night.

In the 1330 Eltham, (Sussex) Closed Rolls 'John de Seint Cler acknowledges that he owes to John de Abernoun, Andrew Maufe and Nicholas del Parke, £1000 to be levied in default of payment of his lands and chattels.

Berwick is a small village situated between Lewes and Polegate. Berwick is recorded in the Domesday Book and was called Berwice meaning 'corn farm'.

On 15th October 1331 Henry Maufe and his wife Joan were licensed to enfeoff Laurence Maufe of a messuage (a building or buildings) 80 acres of land, 4 acres of meadow, 8 acres of wood, 100 acres of heath and four marks rent in Hellyngleye (Hellingly), in Sussex. Held in chief and for him to grant the same to them for their lives with remainder to the right heirs of Joan.

Sussex subsidy Rolls of 1332 lists the following. "At Villat de Ryp (Ripe) Laurenco (Laurence) Maufe 5 shillings and 8¼ pennies; Villat de Excete Andrew Maufee 7 shillings and 9½ pennies; Villat de Brembeltye Andrew Maufe 5 shillings; Villat de Hellynglegh Henry Maufe 11 shillings".

During 1333 Edward III invaded Scotland.

At some time in the reign of Edward III Andrew Maufe is fined at the Kings court in relation to a sore Sparrowhawk. Land in Hellynglegh, also written as Hellingleigh, (Hellingly, Sussex). Hellingly is a village 1½ miles north of Hailsham. Hellingly was involved in the iron industry and had a water mill.

1335. "Grant of all the tenement in Walderne called Posyngwerth which he had of the gift of Margaret daughter of Lord William Heryngod, together with the rents, homages, heriots, reliefs, escheats, etc.

Also of 4 solidates and 5 denariates (legal term realating to land) of rent issuing out of a tenement held of him by John de Meryham at Watere in Walderne. To hold of the capital lords of the fee subject to the services due in respect thereof. Dated at Posyngverth (Possingworth), Thursday next after the feast of the

Annunciation of the
Virgin Mary. — Witnesses :
Lord Andrew Peverel, Nicholas de Beche, and Andrew de Medstede, knights, Andrew Maufee, Henry Maufee, William Cessyngham, Robert de Clavregge, William de Garlaund, Peter de Wylegh, Peter de Hegyngwerth, Geoffrey le Coker, Richard atte Hoke".

1337 saw the out break of war between England and France to become known as The Hundred Years War. This conflict came about when Edward III was expected to pay homage to the king of France for the possessions in France. Edward was averse to doing this because of the French intervention in the Scottish Wars.

Initially England gained the upper hand and destroyed the French fleet at Sluys. A truce was signed after the siege of Tournai in 1340.

The following year France and England were at war over pretensions on Normandy.

In June 1340 an enrolment of deed testified that Andrew Maufee had done homage to Sir Nicholas de la Beche for the lands which he held of him in Alverichston regarding his manor of Chiddyngelegh in Sussex on 13th July in the painted chamber at Westminster in the presence of Sir John de Meere, Peter Gernygal and Edmund de Chelreye.

see page 88

Sir Nicholas de la Beche held immense territories in Berkshire and Sussex. He was appointed governor to the Black Prince. In 1336 he was made Constable of the Tower of London.

In 1343 he was appointed Seneschal (Seneschal; steward or governor of a Medieval Great house) of Gascony. In 1344 he was appointed Govenor of Montgomery Castle.

In 1345 he was sent by the King as commissioner to meet with Alphonso King of Castile about a marriage between the Kings eldest son and Princes Joanna, (Black Prince daughter).
In 1346 whilst the French were trying to invade Guienne Edward landed in Normandy with an army and ravaged the province and also parts of Isle de France and Picardy. The English defeated the French at Crecy and captured Calais.

In 1346 Laurence Maufe and Henry Maufe of Sussex are mentioned in deeds and documents.
'....Laurence Maufe to William le Whyte of the Middlecroft in Chalvington called Betrichturt as enclose by metes and bound to hold of lords of the fee....',
Henry Maufe was a witness.
1348 the Black Death arrived in England and by 1349 it affected the whole country. The plague killed around third of England's population. This helped to break down the barriers of the English language, English replaced French in the courts. The common man started to own land and deeds had to be written for all to understand. Because of the demand for the labour force on the land the common man could negotiate his own wage.
The 1349 and 1350 Papal register for England Ireland, "to Richard Maufee of Westden in the diocese of Chichester. Reservation of a benefice in the gift of the Abbot and Convent of St. Peter's, Gloucester.
France resumed the war by taking St Jean d'Angely in 1351 and defeating the English at St. Omer. In 1355 Edward III invaded Artois while the Black Prince ransacked Languedoc. At the battle of Poitiers in 1356 John of Gaunt was captured and in 1360 the Treaty of

Bretigny was signed.

1361 a new out break of the Black Death arrived in England and lasted until 1362. East Anglia was seriously affected by the pandemic because of the contact with Europe.

1364 Robert Maufe was a witness to an agreement over rent for John Neville at East Farndon.

A Feet of Fines of 1365 for Northamptonshire states "John and Alice have acknowledged the tenements to be the right of William, and have remised and quit claimed 3 shillings, 7 pence and 1 halfpenny of rent from themselves and the heirs of Alice to him and his heirs for ever. And they have granted to William 20 shillings of rent together with the homages and all services of Richard Eenglys, John Kyng, William Bochard', William Bayns, Richard Hume', John Wrangle, John Trauers, Robert Maufe, John son of Henry Clerc', William Aulef' and John Gardyner and their heirs, in respect of all the tenements which they held before of John Neuill' and Alice in the aforesaid vill, (Hardgrave, East Farndon) to hold to William Danet and his heirs, of the chief lords for ever. And besides John and Alice granted for themselves and the heirs of Alice that the moiety - which John Kyng' held for life of the inheritance of Alice in the aforesaid vill on the day the agreement was made for 8 shillings a year, and which after the decease of John Kyng' ought to revert to John Neuill' and Alice and the heirs of Alice - after the decease of John Kyng' shall remain to William and his heirs, to hold together with the rent, of the chief lords for ever'.

The same year, (1365) Robert Maufe paid homage (respect and loyalty) to John Nevill and his wife Alice at East Farndon, Northamptonshire. East Farndon is west of Grafton Underwood and Hemington North of

Northampton. East Farndon is some distance from Hemington and Kingsthorpe, the lands of the Maufe family.

The Nevills were a very influential family. John Neville was 3rd Baron Neville. There could be some confusion with who Alice was. John Neville did not marry Alice but he had a daughter called Alice, also John Nevilles mother was called Alice who was herself from a prominent family, the Audley Family. Alice Audley brother was the Earl of Gloucester, 1st Baron Audley. The Neville family was prominently involved in the Wars of the Roses fighting for and against the king. Nevilles married in to the Plantagenet family during the Wars of the Roses. They owned land through out the north of England including Northamptonshire.

In 1365 Peter I of Cyprus, the Crusading Kingdom launched a Crusade against Egypt. Peter I had spent three years travelling across Europe trying to raise revinue for his Crusade. He also recruited soldiers from France, England and the Holy Roman Empire.

England and France were able to allow soldiers and knights to go on this crusade because of the lull in The Hundred Years War. Many soldiers were idle and had been causing trouble in both countries.

A small contingent volunteered from England that included archers.

The mercenaries Peter I had recruited were led by one of his Barons, Jean de Morphou. He was one of the richest Barons in Cyprus and owned lands in the north of the country around the town of Morphou. Knights Templars also owned land along the coast from Morphou. This region was well known for producing and exporting sugar which was formed in to a bell shape.

The crusade army landed in Alexandra and attacked

the city. The Mamelukes were taken by surprise and the Crusaders were initially successful. Peter I wanted to set up a beach head for reinforcements but many of the mercenaries and foreign barons wanted to leave before the Mamelukes could respond with a counter attack.
There was considerable destruction in Alexandra including the harbour area which affected trade especially with the Genoans, the principle traders from Europe.
The crusaders left after three days with considerable loot.
1369 a new out break of the black death struck England killing a considerable number.
After several years of peace France decided that England had not complied with the Treaty of Bretigny and declared war on England that same year.
In 1369 in the Close Rolls 'Charter of Stephen Randulph, chaplain, giving with warranty to Sir William de Harewell rector of Penhurst, Sussex and Richard Mauffe, their heirs and assigns, all lands, houses, messuages, gardens, arable lands, woods, wood ground, meadows, waters, ponds, hedges, trees, rents, reliefs, escheats, rights etc. in the parish of Penshurst in a place called Hauedenne and in the parish of Chidyngston, as shewn by metes and bounds, which he the said Stephen had of the gift and feoffment of William Coleville.
Dated London, 5 June 37 Edward III. Witnesses: William Salman, John de Haueden', William Sleghtre, Thomas de Esshore, John Morcok'. Close Rolls were a medieval administrative record of letters and deed.
Also in 1369 in the same month 'writing of Stephen Randulf chaplain, rector of Coudenne, being a letter of attorney to Henry atte Sole to deliver to Sir William

Harewell rector of Pensherst and Richard Mauffe seisin of the lands and rights in the parish of Pensherst and Chidyngston which he the said Stephen purchased off William Coleville, as in his charter of feoffment to them contained'.

Dated London, 5 June 1370 Edward III' records show Mauffe also spelt as Mafee.
In 1370 the English were defeated at Pontvallain. After four years and having lost territory Edward III signed the Treaty of Bruges in 1375.
1371 Richard Maufee and Andrew Maufee of Sussex in Dean and Chapter ancient deeds. The deed mentions land formerly of Richard Maufee. Also says Andrew Maufee had sold land. Could the financial burden of the war with France have had some effect on the Maufe/Maufee family.
1372 Peter Mafay mentioned in Customs and Levies as a Gent at Kings Lynn Norfolk.
Peter Mafay had entered in to a trade franchaise.
There are a number of recorded activities such as a 1388 complaint about a Prussian seizure of English merchandise in 1385, the sale of canvas in 1373-74. Sale of lead tiles to the Merchant Guild in 1385-86 and a fine in 1378 for forestalling a tun of oil.
This is the first time a Mafay or Maufe has been refered to as a gent and a member of a Merchant Guild.
Edward III died in 1377 at Sheen and was succeeded by Richard II
France tried to take back French possessions from England but had little success. The King of France Charles V died in 1380.
Charles VI took the throne and there was some reconciliation between the two countries with a period of calm.

In 1385 the men of Kingsthrorpe were granted special priveleges, one was to go toll free any where in England. For such a small hamlet in the middle of the country side this was a considerable privilege.
From Calendar of documents preserved in France. Original Charters in Collection de Bourgoyne (Burgandy), and Cartularies MSS. Lat. 5459, 5458; both in Bibliothèque Nationale, Paris. Relating to Abbey of Cluny, in the Diocese of Macon.

1391. Charter of Stephen, by the grace of God king of the English, addressed generally. He confirms, for his weal and that of his predecessor whatever his barons and other subjects, French and English, have given monastery of St. Pancras,.....(Numerous lands are listed with various barons and knights that have been given before this date going back to 918AD).....
at Ramechinges, 60 acres of land and the marsh belonging to them, of the gift of Hugh de Kahannes; in the same vill 20 acres of land and the marshes belonging to them of the gift of William Malfet; .... of the gift of William Malfet; in Burghurst (Burg ingehurst),..............

ok.
vill = village
where - county

1392 John Mafey entered in Rents as a gent at Kings Lynn, Norfolk. This is tenement of lands. John Mafey is described as to the west of another tenement at Burghard Lane. Another tenement is mentioned as being to the east of John Mafey.
Another entry says of rents and assize at Damgate John Mafey is flanked by Edmund Massyngham. Again a Mafey or Maufe is refered to as a gent. Gentlemen either held land personally or cared for the land and property of the nobility.

Burghorst manor house
(Buckhurst Hill) 69 *Burwash, Sussex*

1393 Richard Maufe rented the manor of Medesey-Maffey, (now Medesey-Burton, Eastbourne, Sussex 1395 record of Richard Maufe and a rental made in Eastbourne, Sussex.

To encourage peace between France and England Richard II was to marry the daughter of Charles VI in 1396 but Richard died at Pontefract Castle in 1400. Henry IV succeeded to the throne and hostilities resumed.

15th Century

The changes to the English language during the 14th century carried on during the 15th century. Spelling and pronounciation changed for vowels and words.
The printed press brought further changes with various published works by people such as Chaucer.

1400 Richard II died at Pontefract Castle and was succeeded by Henry IV.
1403 Richard Maufe is one of the witness's to a document.
1408 a Sussex record mentions Richard Maufe in deeds and documents dated 22nd September.
'……By Thomas Sakevyle, knight to Richard Maufe, Thomas Wallere senr, John Brook and Nicholas Selwyn of the site of the Manor at Chalvyngton and also and tenements, rent and services etc. with all their rights, liberties and appurts, in the county of Sussex, which are held by the king immediately within the Rape of Pevensey. To hold for life of the grantees they doing to the lords of the fee the rents and services therefore due and accustomed. Warrant….'
Again at this late date we see a member of the Sackville family in the same document as a Maufe.

A London record dated 1413, "She held in fee tail 2 messuages, 9 shops with solars above, 5 cottages with chambers and a wharf in the parish of All Hallows the Great. William Tarent, Walter Mydilton, clerk, and Richard Mauffe held these premises in their demesne (held in legal right) as of fee and granted them to Nicholas Loveyn, knight, and Margaret then his wife then hold to them and the heirs of their bodies. Their daughter Margaret married

Richard Chaumberleyn and had issue (son) Richard". Richard the father died and Margaret married Philip Seincler (Sinclaire) a knight, and had two sons, John and Thomas. Richard the son is next heir of Margaret'. All Hallows the Great was recorded as early as 1100. A church here was referred to as All Hallowed of Thames Street, All Hallows of Hay and All Hallows of Ropery. The last two names refered to the hay sold near by on the Hay Warfe and the ropes made on a near by street. The church was not far from London Bridge. The original church was burnt down in the Great Fire of London.

1413, Henry IV died at Westminster Palace and was succeeded by Henry V.

The treaty between England and France expired and in 1415 Henry V landed in Normandy with a large army with the intention to invade Normandy. Henry's army was successful after capturing Harfleur, Rouen, St. Lo along with other cities in Normandy falling to the invading army.

The English defeated the French at the Battle of Agincourt after that the French were reluctant to engage the English on the battle field.

The cities were pillaged by the invading English Army, taking every thing from treasures to live stock. Children were said to be taken and sent back to England and sold as servants, but most likely treated as slaves. Other cities, towns and castles fell, some were just handed over to Henry in fear of being killed. Henrys invasion was vicious, killing many who resisted.

Henry introduced a policy of colonisation. Those of any standing in England were encouraged to settle in Normandy, they were given land that had been vacated by the French nobility who hid out in the countryside. They were also given titles, similar to what William I of

England did after invading in 1066.
Henry encouraged English soldiers and gentry to marry in to the Norman families who then inherited the property and land. Those that accepted to settle were obliged to stay in Normandy and not return to England under the threat of being killed if they did. Marshalls were installed to ensure no one fled back to England, but many did after being raided and settlers killed by the landless French knights and nobility who had resorted to begging or stealing. Some took menial work in establishments such as kitchens and inn's.
Having conquered Normandy Henry set his sights on invading France and claimed to be the heir to the French throne. This invasion was equally vicious with many French being massacred, the land was wasted and villages burnt as the army marched through France. Henry is quoted to saying "an invasion requires burning like sausage requires mustard".
Henry instilled extreme discipline in his army. There was no excuse to surrender or run from a battle, even for his family. Those that did were killed with extreme brutality.
One soldier in a foraging party ran away when the others were killed by raiding French soldiers. The individual having escaped the French was duly punished, he was buried alive under Henry's orders. Henry was equally feared by his nobles, knights and men at arms.
After capturing Paris Henry V was offered the hand of Catherine, the King of France daughter with the titles regent and heir to the kingdom of France.
Having taken Meaux on the 2nd of May 1429 Henry ceremoniously entered Paris on the 30th of May. Henry invaded further south but died on the 31st of August in the Bois de Vincennes.

Henry VI succeeded to the throne and was successful against France with its new king. After England had taken a number of French Cities France was on the verge of surrendering. Joan de Arc then helped lead the French in a number of successful victories forcing the English back towards the coast as cities fell. In 1444 Henry VI signed the treaty of Tours which gave Normandy land back to France.

In 1450 there was a Rebellion in the South East England. The ring leader was Jack Cade. The rebellion was in opposition to the people of Kent being accused of the death of Earl of Suffolk.

The Earl of Suffolk had been murdered whilst sailing to France under a letter of safe passage. He had been accused of being responsible for the treaty of Troyes because the land in Normandy was handed back.

There were also up risings in Sussex, Surrey and Essex led by respectable gentlemen. A number of rebels marched on London and several prominent people were executed by the rebels.

After several days those who had revolted were given a pardon, they returned home but the pardons were rescinded. Jack Cade was run to ground at Heathfield in Sussex and died his wounds he received resisting capture. Others were also punished for their part which included having their land attainted, (confiscated).

There was a subsequent rebellion in Sussex which brought retribution against those who took part.

England lost more territory to France and cities surrendered until being expelled from Normandy in 1453.

The English were left in small enclave of Calais which became known as the English Pale. This was held until 1558.

1455 saw the out break of the Wars of the Roses, a

bitterly fought series of campaigns and battles for control of England between the York and Lancastrian Houses. It was to last until 1485.

The first battle of this war at St. Albans involved the Lancastrian army led by King Henry VI, also a Noble Man, the 1st Duke of Buckingham. They marched out of London to meet the Yorkists Barons at St. Albans. The smaller Lancastrian army was defeated and the king was captured by the Yorkists. Many of the Lancastrian nobles were killed in the battle. The Duke of Buckingham was wounded but survived.

Through the king the Yorkists controlled England in their favour rewarding themselves with land and titles. The 1st Duke of Buckingham owned land through out the Midlands and the South. Buckingham's retainers from Sussex, Surrey and Kent were unable to make it to St. Albans in time for the battle but were still paid. Of all of Buckingham's properties he preferred to live at Tonbridge, Kent. In the Domesday Book Tonbridge was written as 'Tonebrige', an Anglo Saxon name. Tonbridge was a market town. The River Medway was forded at Tonbridge until a bridge was built in 1191. A castle was built in the 11th century by Richard Fitz Gilbert. Until 1870 Tonbridge was written as Tunbridge but the name was changed by the post office to save confusion with Tunbridge Wells not too far away. Buckingham also owned land and property in Bletchingley, Surrey. A manor was held for him by Henry Hextall and known as 'Hextalls' at Little Pickle. This manor does not stand any more but there is a moated area. Bletchingley appears in the Domesday Book of 1086 as 'Blachingelei'. Bletchingley held some importance until the 14th century as a borough but Reigate gradually became a town and lost it's importance.

Another of the many estates and land held by The Duke of Buckingham in the Southern and Middle Counties in England was Bridgnorth in Shropshire. Part of the estate was Morfé Forest, the previously mentioned forest frequented by the Kings of England. Morfe Forest is close to Wenlock Abbey.
Henry Hextall was a courtier to The Duke of Buckingham and a land owner in Staffordshire. He also held manors at Barden and Hadlow in Tonbridge. Thomas Hextall was to become Custodian of Dover and mayor of Dover. He was tried for assisting Duke of Warwick on his return from Calais but was pardoned.
In 1459 a Lancastrian army was raised to reinstall the King. The Earl of Salisbury's Yorkist army defeated the Lancastrians at Blore Heath. The two armies met again at Ludford Bridge, after which the Lancastrian leaders went in to exile, their land and property was attainted, (confiscated).

In 1460 the Lancastrians gathered another army but again were defeated by the Duke of Warwick at Northampton where the 1st Duke of Buckingham was killed.
There were further battles at Wakefield and Mortemers Cross but no southerners seem to have been involved in these battles. The Duke of Buckinghams land and property was attainted and distributed between Warwicks followers.
We can assume because the Duke of Buckingham fought at Northampton retainers from Sussex or Surrey were present and maybe Maufes fought as well.
An attempt at negotiations broke out in to another round of battles. The Second Battle of St. Albans in 1461 had the
Yorkist army led by Warwick, the Duke of Norfolk was

Edward IV becoming king

also present with retainers from Norfolk and Suffolk. At this time the Yorkists also held Henry VI prisoner. The Lancastrians defeated the Yorkist Army and rescued Henry. Kentish troops with Warwick allegedly defected to the Lancastrian army. This battle saw the massacring of common soldiers and the beheading of the nobility, including knights.

~~At Towton~~ Edward IV fought the Lancastrians and defeated them. *at Towton* After the battle of Towton there were a number of Lancastrian rebellions which were put down. In 1464 another Lancastrian army took to the field. Edward IV responded and Warwick's brother defeated the Lancastrian Army and captured Henry VI and Queen Margaret. This followed with massacres and executions that put down any fresh revolt.

Edward ruled peacefully until Warwick with the rest of his family turned against Edward but were forced to go in to exile in France. Edward confiscated land and property of 53 of Warwick's supporters.

Warwick returned with Burgundian Mercenaries and some retainers. He sailed to Yorkshire then marched to Wakefield to gather more support where he had retainers. He marched south and other noblemen rallied to him.

1471 saw an out break of Black Death that killed as much as 10-15% of the population.

That same year Warwick's army met the Kings under Montagu, Warwick's brother, at Barnet. In the confusion of battle both Warwick and Montagu were killed. Henry VI was captured again and taken to the Tower of London.

The same year Margaret of Anjou landed in the west and rallied North Welsh allies. Edward marched with a fresh army from Windsor. The two armies met at Tewkesbury and Margaret's army was defeated.

Edward, her son was killed and sixteen of her noblemen were executed.

This was the last battle Edward IV fought and he consolidated his reign with the exception of several minor rebellions.

There was a second out break of the Black Death in 1479 killing as much as 20% of the population.

That same year Henry VI died at Tower of London Edward IV succeeded Henry but died in 1483, his son Edward V became King. Richard Duke of Gloucester was his guardian but mysteriously Edward V and his brother vanished, rumoured to have died. They were to be known as the Two Princes in the Tower.

Richard Duke of Gloucester who married Anne Neville was crowned Richard III. Richard was popular at first until it was rumoured that he had killed the two princes.

The 2nd Duke of Buckingham who had been a loyal supporter of Richard rebelled against him in 1483 Henry Tudor who was exiled in Brittany was to cross the channel with a small army and meet up with Buckingham.

Across the south of England all of the counties rebelled, from Kent to Cornwall and minor rebellions rose up in East Anglia.

Buckingham raised an army in Wales but was unable to meet up with the rebels in England hampered by the bad weather. The River Servern was un-crossable resulting in the rebel army fading away.

Richard commissioned the Earl of Surrey to lay siege to Bodiam Castle in Sussex. The rebels surrendered with out any resistance. Also several armies were mobilised across the Midlands. Buckingham hid with trusted supporters but was betrayed and captured. Richard III had Buckingham executed in Salisbury, his lands, estates and property across Central and Southern England were attainted (confiscated).

Even so Richard died pardoned and offered immunity to Yeoman and those of lower standing saying they had been deceived and blinded.

One of the main beneficiaries of this attainment was John Howard, the Duke of Norfolk. Richard III gave John estates and manors in Surrey, Sussex as well as Huntingdonshire, Essex, Norfolk and Suffolk. This added to his already extensive holdings in Surrey, Sussex, Norfolk and Suffolk. John Howard was also made master forester to all of the lands that was held by Buckingham.

Those who rebelled in the south had their land and properties attainted and lost their titles, which in many cases were given when Richard came to the throne. Those who took part in the rebellion included nobility, knights, esquires, gentry, merchants and lawyers. They held titles such as receivers, sheriffs and peace commissioners

Many of those who took part and who were suspected of aiding and supporting the rebellion were indicted for high treason, a crime that automatically carried the death after the Treason Act of 1351. The statutory sentence was to be hung, drawn and quartered.

Many others had their lands confiscated, no body was to be trusted, not even the clergy who were accused of aiding rebels.

The rebels had the opportunity to plead for a pardon or as was the case at the time buy a pardon.

The extent of anticipation for being suspected of being involved in the rebellion resulted in some asking for a pardon as a precausion. People such as William Caxton who was an associate of the Earl Rivers. Arch Deacons were suspected of harbouring rebels as well as other individuals, these included the Archbishop of York and the Bishop of London.

Many chose to go in to exile in France, joining Henry Tudor in Brittany. Even servants in the service of the rebellion leaders were forbidden to be retained by any one else.

3 Bishops were involved, several senior churchmen were implicated

Richard III felt insecure after these rebellions considering Buckingham was a close and trusted Duke. This rebellion became to be known as 'Buckingham's Rebellion'.

On 23rd 1484 Parliament met at Westminster and passed an act of attainder. Convicting the conspiritors through out England of High Treason and forfeiture of all of their estates.

Robert Brakynbury, esquire of the Royal Body and Constable of the Tower of London was appointed as Receiver General. He was responsible for taking in to the Hands of the Crown by forfeiture or otherwise estates in Sussex, Surrey and Kent.

Richard brought many of his loyal Northern Barons, Earls, Knights and Esquires south and they virtually colonised the counties along the south coast, from Kent to Cornwall. They were granted land and properties that had been confiscated, especially of those who had fled to France. Even those who had been pardoned did not regain their titles but were given enough land to farm and support their families, becoming farmers over night.

Robert Brachenbury, born in County Durham received land in Kent Surrey and Sussex, as did many other of Richards's supporters. Manors in Surrey went to Sir John Neville whilst John Howard the Duke of Norfolk received the submissions of those in the East of the Southern Counties.

This caused resentment in the shires when the Northern nobles and their retainers took over governing and administrating the southern counties. They controlled where individuals could go and with whom they could meet.

Rebels had to have guarantors and were told where to live. It was to become known as 'The Northern

Any one connected with Richard through his household as his feoffer, his estate office, lawyers and retainers. Also those who served Northumberland, Nevilles and other Northern lords

Crowland, a chronicle of the time mentions the "Tyrannical imposition of Northerners against Southerners.

Tyranny', the Northern Lords governed as they liked in Richards name.

After John Howard was granted the esates of the Duke of Buckingham he toured those in Sussex and Surrey. Howards influence in these two counties was paramount, most probably because of the anticipated invasion by Henry Tudor. John Howard was also the sub-admiral of Suffolk and Norfolk where he apprehended pirates raiding along the East Coast. Several pirates he had caught came from the south coast.

Richard was not sure where Henry Tudor might try to land and positioned his supporters strategically along the South and South East coast. He increasingly whilst exiled in France gained popularity in Wales. In 1485, after being given financial and military support by France Henry sailed to Wales and landed at Milford Haven. Henry's small French force and retainers were joined by loyal supporters in Wales as his army marched east.

Richard's and Henry's armies met at Bosworth. The bitter battle looked as if it would go Richard's way. Stanley arrived during the battle with his force and instead of joining Richard sided with Henry. At the same time the Duke of Northumberland's large force, Richard III reserve failed to engage the enemy. Richard charged at Henry but was left making a last stand fighting courageously. Richard III was killed and the battered crown was retrieved and given to Henry Tudor on the battle field.

Others in Richards army were also killed, the Duke of Norfolk and Sir Robert Brackenbury, The Earl of Surrey (Duke of Norfolk's son) was captured and held in the Tower of London. The Duke of Northumberland who did not commit his troops was captured and imprisoned.

Henry Tudor was crowned in London and became Henry VII.

All of the battles of the Wars of the Roses were north of the River Thames, the southern counties and East Anglia managed to carry on with their daily lives.

Before the Wars of the Roses the Maufe name in Northamptonshire had died out. Very few records exist but across East Anglia and in Shropshire Morphew and Morphewe start to appear. In Surrey where the Duke of Buckingham held land there is a similar picture and Morphews can be found in the same area as the Maufes and on land previously owned by Maufes. The same land Richard III gave to his Northern supporters to govern.

Richards's supporter's accents from the Northern counties would have sounded very strange to those of the far south. Equally the Southern accents would have sounded peculiar to these northerners. 'Maufe or Maufee' when pronounced could easily be mistaken as 'Morphew', the skin affliction which would have caused some amusement with Richards Northern supporters. The Duke of Buckingham was originally from the north and again could have mistaken Maufe for Morphew. Today the Normandy village of la Meauffe is pronounced as 'Me uf', 'Mouf' or 'Moof ai'.

After the Battle of Bosworth the crown retained a number of confiscated knightly and noble lands, as well as esquires, clerics, yeoman and merchants. Henry VII as an act of parliament attainted Richard III and his men taking control of their land and property.

After the Wars of the Roses a member of the Carrington Family changed his name to Smith to avoid imprisonment, as others did.

The Earl of Surrey was released from the Tower of London by Henry VII to help quall rebellions in the north and stop raids from Scotland in the north of England. He was given his lands back in return for support. The Duke of Northumberland was released and but was killed by citizens in York who had revolted against taxes imposed by Henry.

Through out the Wars of the Roses lands were confiscated from families who happened to be on the wrong side and then restored. But it depended how powerful an individual was. The most powerful were dealt with first whilst those of a lower rank had to wait longer. Some even had to wait until the reign of Henry VIII before having their land restored to their family.

A good proportion of the rebels who took part in The Duke of Buckinghams Rebellion in Sussex, Surrey and Kent were pardoned but they did not get back their land. Richard III directed that all of those in Kent were to take an oath of allegiance to him.

We have to consider the death toll during the campaign's and battles. Most of the dead on both sides were English making the burden higher than that of campaigns in France. As the Wars of the Roses dragged on for the thirty years the battles became more vicious. Many prisoners were executed, including the ordinary foot soldier. It is possible Maufe's also died in battle or possibly executed.

Armies during this time were banded together at short notice from different counties by the military leaders. Foreign Mercenaries mixed with those of the North of England, the Southern Counties and West Country. All had their own accents, in Wales and Cornwall they had their own language.

The Duke of Buckingham owned land through out the Midlands, the South and South East, From the Wash in

the East to the Severn in the West and Wales. He was Lord Warden of the Cinque Ports in Sussex and Kent. When land and property was attainted from a noble man all those under him would loose their land as well. Families were left without any income. Some became destitute over night and had to work doing menial tasks. Retainers were known to move from one lord to another when circumstances suited, Hastings retainers moved to the Duke of Buckingham after Hastings was executed.
Maufes along with others would have had land attainted when the Duke of Buckingham was executed.

1487 also1489 to 1490 there are records of Thomas Morphewe renting rooms in Winchester. Thomas Morphewe was a Farmer's Guild Merchant
being able to buy and sell farmers merchandise. To belong to a guild you had to have some standing in society and some wealth.
Winchester had always been an important place. The treasury was held here since the Anglo Saxon times until Henry VIII moved it to London. At one time it was an important centre for the wool tradel. The Italians (Lombards) and Spanish amongst others bought the wool. English wool was considered the best in Europe. Through out the Middle Ages the King owned all of the wool in England and controlled the price.
Winchester was also where the long pilgrimage to Canterbury started for those who arrived from countries and Kingdoms in Western and Southern Europe, the pilgrimage was for St. Thomas Becket, the Archbishop killed in Canterbury Catherdral in 1170 by knights of Henry II. The Pilgrims followed the 'Pilgrim Way', a trail that led towards the South Downs on the edge of the Weald of Sussex. The road would then travel north in

to Surrey, south of London in to Kent then down to Canterbury and the Cathedral. A long journey that could be fraught with danger, especially for wealthy foreigners (strangers)

Also in 1489 there were a number of rebellions in regions that were not in total allegiance to Henry VII, this made Henry build up his army.

Foreign gun makers were invited to England. In 1496 Henry authorised and financed a new iron works at Newbridge in the Sussex Weald. This was the first recorded blast furnace in England. This blast furnace manufactured cannon-balls and iron fittings for gun carriages.

The iron was extracted from the ground by digging large open pits. The damp ore was melted down in the furnace using charcoal which burns at a higher temperature than wood.

The whole process involved considerable manpower. Digging the pit for the iron ore, cutting the wood for making charcoal. Gullies were dug to collect water behind dams for the water wheel which operated the furnace bellow.

1498, there is a record of Richard Maflay in the Sussex wills.

Through out the 15th century there were several rebellions in the south. From the one led by Jack Cade to the Duke of Buckinghams rebellion. Many had their land attainted. It is possible at some time the Maufe's would be affected by one of these rebellions and be attainted, even if they were not involved.

16th Century

The changes in the English language continued during the 16th century. Henry VIII published the English Bible so everyone could read it in church.

Various works by authors and playwrites developed the language but there still was no standard spelling, words were spelt as they seemed to be spelt. Shakespear's name was spelt eighty different ways and he also spelt his own name differently on six occasions.

It is difficult finding any Morphews in Sussex during the 16th century. They lived predominantly in Suffolk, Norfolk and Surrey. Maufe's are recorded in Sussex at the start of the centuy in legal documents relating to land, but soon after this the Maufe name cannot be traced. There is an A. Maufe in Norfolk who died circa 1596 and a John Maufe dying in 1538 in West Yorkshire.

So few Morphews in Sussex could be attributed to Maufe's being attainted by Richard III in 1483. Having to move out of the county owing to the sensitivety of being potential rebels near the coast where Henry Tudor (Henry VII) might land.

In the 16th century the Maufe name seems to die out. There are very few records of Maufe post 1500 that involves ownership of land in Sussex. The Morphew name appears in records where none can be found pre Wars of the Roses.

As well as Morphew a Morphewe spelling is found most notably in Pulham, Norfolk in burial records. Pulham was in the Hundred of Earsham which was wholly at the liberty of the Duke of Norfolk during the middle ages. Earsham Manor was retained by the Earl of Norfolk for his ancestors and was granted by Richard I and Henry II. Pulham is mentioned in the Domesday

Book where it was refered to as Pollcham.
The countryside around Pullham is flat, fields are interspersed by country lanes. A 19th century map shows very little has changed in over a hundred years. The Morphewe spelling is also found in some other county parish records.
Between 1507 and 1508 there is another record of a John Morphew renting a room in Winchester.
Henry VII died in 1509 at Richmond Palace and was succeeded by Henry VIII.
At the start of Henrys reign he placed orders with the Iron Masters in the Weald. Furnaces established themselves across Sussex and in Kent. By 1513 a large quantity of gunstones (cannon-balls) were delivered

A Sussex document dated 1512 records 'John Maufe V William Maufe manors of Eghenton, Claverham, and Chitinglegh and advowson of church of the same manor of Chitynlegh. William remit to John the advowson and ¾ of manors of Claverham and Chityngleg with reversion of manor of Eghenton and other third of manors of Claverham and Chitynglegh which Joan late wife of William Maufe holds in dower for which John gives William 200 marks'.
The English army invaded Scotland and defeated the Scottish Army at Flodden in 1513.
'1515 Nicholas de la Beche v John Maufe; two thirds of manor of Claverham, (Sussex), to Nicholas for 200 marks'.
'1516 Bartholemew de Badlesmere (by Adam de Brom) v John Maufe; manor of Eyghinton which Joan late the wife of William Maufe holds in dower; reversion of the manor to Bartholomew for £80

1520 John Maufe v William Maufe; two-third of manor at Chitinglegh; to John for life, with remainder to Nicholas de la Beche and his heirs'. The Maufe family still holds land in Chittingley at this date but Nicholas de la Beche is being given part of the property for some reason.

1521 Nicholas de le Beche v John Maufe; third of manors of Chitinglegh and Claverham which Joan late the wife of William Maufe holds in dower; reversion of said third to Nicholas for 100 marks.

The previous four records of John Maufe are interesting. It is obviously about land and property the Maufe family hold in Sussex. William Maufe is deceased and his wife (widow) holds the deeds in dowery and has not agreed to the sale and wants them returned. The two gentlemen involved in the case, Nicholas de la Beche and Bartholomew de Badlesmere appear to be impostures. These two eminent families were close to Edward I and Edward II. Nicholas de la Beche left no heirs. Bartholemew de Badlesmere had his lands attainted after rebelling. Maybe these individuals were chancing their arm and land jumping by pretending to be someone more important than they really were. Adam de Brom again was someone closely connected to Edward II who originated from Suffolk.

Either way these characters appear to gain financially by being paid for the reversal of the transactions on a considerable amount of land. We also see Maufe's still owned land Chittingleigh.

These two properties were in the area that iron ore was being dug out of the ground, maybe the court cases were the reason for the interest shown in the properties. By 1520 iron production was escalating

across the Weald. This resulted in expert
Iron workers being brought in from France.
A 1537 record shows a John Morphew being
pensioned off at Wenlock Abbey in Shropshire. Henry
VIII reformation caused England to split from the
Vatican and Henry VIII set up the Church of England.
Wenlock Abbey, along with many other Abbey's at the
time of the reformation were demolished and all its
property confiscated. Wenlock Abbey, Priory was under
the Cluniac Order of monks. The Cluniac church was
invited to England from France by William I who
donated considerable sums to the church.
The Cluniac Order devoted them selves to prayer and
hired others to work on their land.
A record from 1537 shows a John Morphew from
Halstead, Essex married into a wealthy family in
Dedham, (John Constable Country).
Halstead is situated on a steep hill with a river running
through it. The countryside surrounding Halstead
comprises of arable fields with several small copse.
Halstead has been occupied since the early Bronze
Age. A village was situated here during the Roman
occupation. It was recorded in the Domesday Book. A
grammar school was founded here in 1594.
William Levett a Royal gunstone maker. In 1543 built a blast furnace at Buxted with the intention to
cast an iron cannon. This was successful and a foundry
with two blast furnaces was established.
The Royal Navy requested cannons to be made for its
ships as well as iron cannon balls. The English
Cannons of this time were considered the best in
Europe and other countries wanted to buy them.
Buxted was one of the prominent places in the Weald
where iron was smelted and forged at the blast
furnaces. The first blast furnace was established in

1491 at Hoggets Farm.

In 1584 there were complaints about streams being diverted, roads being damaged by the heavy wagons carrying the iron ore, iron and charcoal. Queen Elizabeth's government passed a law requiring the sixth wagon to carry gravel to resurface the road.

By 1549 53 forges were operating in the Weald. The iron industry doubled over the next 25 years, by 1574 there were 110 furnaces and forges in the Weald. About 1540 there is a baptism record of John Marphe (Morfeive) at Bletchingley in Surrey. In 1564 John married Annye (Amye) Kelycke at Blechingley. They had four children, all baptised at Bletchingly. John Morfeive 1575, Nicholas Morfeive 1571, Richard Morfeive 1578 and Thomas Morfey.

Bletchingley village is up on the Surrey South Downes where the old 'Pilgrim Way' passed through from Winchester to Canterbury. Fire Stone and Hearth Stone was quarried here at this time for important constructions such as Windsor Castle and in London such as Westminster Abbey for the font.

Bletchingley Palace or Manor was here, a great Tudor House which **Anne of Cleves** occupied after her marriage to **Henry VIII** was annulled 1540. Anne also received Richmond Palace on the River Thames. Neither of these Grande Buildings exists today.

1547 Henry VIII died at the Palace of Whitehall and was succeeded by Edward VI. Edward died in 1553 at Greenwich Palace. He was succeeded by his sister Mary to become Mary I.

Mary was a devout Catholic and tried to reverse the reformation and bring England back under the Vatican. Entries in the Parish records were written in Latin again

1558 Mary I died and was succeeded by Elizabeth I. Her reign was to become known as the Elizabethan Era.

From 1571 there are records of Morphews living in the villages of Blechingley, Merstham, Godstone and Gatton all within a few miles of each other in the Redhill/Reigate area.

Nicholas Morfewe born 1571, place unknown married Mary Persivall at Merstham, Surrey in 1612.

In the 16th century Sussex was to come in to prominence as a centre of Englands iron industry. The area known as the Weald of Surrey, Sussex and Kent has rich deposits of iron in the clay, this had been extracted since Roman times where the Weald supplied much of the iron for the Roman Army in England.

There is mention in the Domesday Book of the Iron Industry in Sussex. There is evidence of Medieval Bloomeries that were used for produced horse shoes and nails. Records show orders for Archbishop of Canterbury in 1242 and the Sheriff of Sussex in 1253. In 1496 blast furnaces were introduced in the north of Sussex operated by skilled Flemish immigrant workers, replacing the primitive Bloomeries. Iron out put went from a few kilos to near a tonne.

A Large number of people were employed felling trees for the charcoal, digging pits to extract the iron clay and transporting the iron.

The country side around Buxted is undulating fileds and woodland. The woodland was extensive in the 16th century before much of it was felled for building Royal Navy ships and making charcoal for the blast furnaces. Morphews are found in the village of Hoxne, an ancient village half mile south of the River Waveney. Hoxne is mentioned in the Domesday Book. In 1535 the manor

passed to the King, Hnery VIII.
In 1588 Spain sent a large fleet to invade England. This became known as the Spanish Armada. The planned invasion failed with many Spanish ships lost in the storm that beset the fleet in the English Channel
In 1592 England sent 200 cannons to the Dutch for their war against the Spanish.

In High Hurstwood, Uckfield, Sussex there is a 16th century cottage that still stands today. It is called Morphews Cottage but was originally called Morphee Cottage. This is of archaeological significance, ancient bloomery's have been discovered near by. 19th century contemporary maps of the area show the fields backing on to the property also called 'Morphews'.
From about the same time there is a 'Morphew Cottage' in Nedging road, Nedging Tye, Suffolk near Ipswich, close to Constable Country.

Norfolk Morphew, Morfew and Morphewe

Johan Morphewe: 1551 burial Pulham.
Alyce (Alice) Morphewe: 1552 burial Pulham.
Jo Morphewe: 1556 burial Pulham.
Alyce (Alice) Morphewe: 1557 burial Pulham.
Bridget Morphewe: 1560 marriage Great Moulton with Little Moulton.
Richard Morphewe: 1561 burial Pulham
John Morphewe: 1568 burial Pulham.
Robert Morphewe: 1568 burial Pulham
John Morphew: 1572 married, Yaxby, East Anglia
Will Morfew: 1574 marriage, place unknown
Honor Morphewe: 1576 burial Pulham.
Robert Morphewe: 1576 burial Pulham.
Elizabeth Morphewe: 1576 buried Pulham.

Elizabeth Morphewe: 1577 burial Pulham
Thomas Morfew: 1578 marriage, place unknown.
William Morphewe: 1579 marriage Great Moulton with Little Moulton.
Marye Morphew: 1579 baptised, Forncett St Peter.
Alice Morphewe: 1581 burial Pulham.
Jeffrey Morphewe: 1582 burial Pulham.
Roger Morfew: 1582 place unkown.
Rebecca Morphewe, baptised 1583, Pulham St. Mary.
Rebecca Morphewe: 1583 burial Pulham
Maidchild Morphewe: 1584 burial Pulham.
Richard Morphew, 1584 baptised, Pulham St. Mary
Peter Morphew, 1584 baptised, Pulham St. Mary
Roger Morphewe, 1585 baptised, Pulham St Mary.
Alicea Morphew, 1585 baptised, Pulham St. Mary
Roger Morphewe: 1585 burial Pulham.
John Morphew, 1586 baptised, Pulham St. Mary.
William Morphew, 1587 baptised, Pulham St. Mary.
Philip Morphew, 1587/88 baptised, Pulham St. Mary.
Joseph Morphew, 1589/90 baptised, Pulham St. Mary.
Rogerus Morphewe: 1592 baptism, Thelveton.
Elizabeth Morphew, 1596 baptised, Pulham St. Mary.
Peter Morphewe: 1598 burial, Pulham.

Suffolk Morphew, Morfew and Morphewe

Mary Morfew: 1561, marriage, place unknown. Norfolk and Suffolk record.
John Morphewe: 1564 married Grace Jonys on 4th May at Hoxne, in Suffolk Pipe Rolls.
John Morfew: 1564 marriage, place unknown.
Richard Morphew: recorded at Rawlton.
John Morphewe in 1568 Suffolk Parish Registers
George Morphew: buried, Hoxne, date unknown
Oliver Selfe: 1577 married Mary Morfewe on 15th September, Hoxne.
John Morfew: 1577 marriage, place unknown.
Mary Morfew: 1577 marriage, Forncett St. Peter.
Elizabeth Morfew: 1577 marriage, place unknown.
Ann Morphewe: 1582 burial Westleton.
George Morfew: 1584 marriage, place unknown
Jedian Morphew: 1594 married Margaret Prentice at Palgrave, Suffolk. Margaret was born in 1567 at Trandston, Suffolk.
John Morfew: 1599 marriage, place unkown.

Surrey Morphew

John Morphe (Morfeive), Morfeiue: born c. 1540 Blechingley died 1612. The 'V' is the latin 'U'.
John Morphe (Morfeive): married Annye (Any) Kelycke in 1564 at Blechingley.
Benedict Morphewe: 1568 is recorded at Hoxted (Oxted?).
John Morfee: 1575 baptised, Gatton.

Nicholas Morfeive (Morfeiue): born 1571 at Blechingley, died 1612, parents John and Annye Morfeive.

John Morfeive (Morfeiue): born 1575 Blechingley, married Margaret Pitter, parents John and Annye Morfeive.

Richard Morfeive (Morfeiue): born 1578 Blechingley, parents John and Annye Morfeive.

Thomas Morfey: born 1581 Blechingley, parents John and Annye Morfeive.

Darthy/Dorothy Morffye/Morphew. Recorded at the Rose and Crown, Southwark over several years 1591-1593. Each year was written separately. Some hand writing is difficult to read because of the style of the hand.

This was at the time when the Rose Theatre was built on Rose Ally in Soutwark on Bankside, as well as the Globe, Swan and Hope Theatres. Shakespearian plays were being performed in the Rose Theatre before the Globe was built. Much of Soutwark was burnt down in the Great Fire of Soutwark which was more devistating than the Great Fire of London.

Today there is a Rose and Crown pub not far from London Bridge and Southwark Catherdral.

In 1592 there was a severe out break of Bubonic plague which lasted until 1593.

John Morphew: Married Margaret Pitter at Merstham 1599.

17th Century

1603 Queen Elizabeth I died at Richmond Palace, Surrey ending the Tudor period. She is succeeded by James I (James VI of Scotland) and starting the reign of the Stuarts.

The iron industry in the Weald of Sussex went from strength to strength manufacturing cannons for the Royal Navy to arm the ever larger ships.

The army benefited as well with what was considered the best cannons in Europe.

The Morphews in Surrey moved from Bletchingley to Merstham where Green Stone was being quarried for building work in London. The stone had been mined for several centuries and was used for Henry VIII Nonsuch Palace in Surrey.

In Suffolk Morphews still congregated at Hoxne, a village near the Suffolk Coast.

In Norfolk there are a number of records of Morphewe's in Dickleburgh with Langmere. Originally it was recorded as Dickleburgh and was part of the Hundred of Diss. The manor was owned at one point by John and Thomas Whipple, John Whipple were from Pulham where Morphew's were recorded in the previous century.

During the reign of James I there was the Gun Powder Plot, an attempt to blow up the Houses of Parliament, this was foiled and the instigators were executed.

James I died in 1625 and was succeeded by his son Charles I. Charles reign was beset by his disagreement with Parliament. This resulted in the First English Civil War of 1642 – 1646.

There were several battles but when the financial resources ran out Charles went to Scotland to seek help but Charles was handed over to Parliament.

Charles was imprisoned but this left a power vacuum which the Scots took advantage of and invaded England with the intention of putting Charles I back on the throne.

This led to the Second English Civil War lasting from 1648 – 1649. There were a number of battles and sieges with the Royalists being defeated. A number of nobles were executed along with Charles at Whitehall Palace.

In 1649 Royalist supporters rallied with Charles II as their leader. There were up risings in Ireland and Scotland. The Royalist army met the Parliamentarians at Worcester in 1651. Charles army was defeated and he escaped to France.

An interesting note to the English Civil War was settlers returned from the Colonies in Virginia (America) to fight in the war.

In 1660 Matthew Morphew was made a Knight of the Royal Oak. Charles II awarded those who supported him whilst he was in exile. Charles II was advised not to create the new Order incase it caused animosity with Parliament. Instead he gave one person from each parish a sum that reflected the value of their property, Matthew Morphew was awarded £1000. Matthew Morphew at the time was living in Worcestershire.

1664 the Hearth Tax was introduced against any house or dwelling with more than two hearths (fire places). A record shows a Hen Morphew was levied hearth tax on a property in Tandridge Hundred, Surrey.

In 1665 there was the Great Plague of London that lasted until the following year.

Captain Brian Morfey or Morphey was called to give evidence, along with other defendeants (Finan, Callaghan and Moyer) who lived in Ireland at the time.

They are mentioned in a long letter saying they are returning to Ireland but not in custody but to give evidence against Archbishop Oliver Plunkett, who was charged with plotting a French invasion, (a Popish Plot).

Having defeated the Irish in 1653 Cromwell banned the Catholic faith. Archbishop Plunkett had returned from Rome and preached in Ireland. He went in to hiding but still practiced his faith whilst travelling in disguise. Archbishop Plunkett was first tried in Ireland but the judiciary could not find a jury that was considered trustworthy. Plunkett was moved to Newgate Prison in 1681 and tried in London. He was found guilty and sentenced to be hung, drawn and quartered.

Charles II died in 1685 at Whitehall Palace. He was succeeded by James II who was deposed in 1688 and succeeded by William III, William of Orange and Mary II. Mary died in 1694.

The 17th century saw the iron and cannon production in the Weald increase, the early sparks that were to later ignite the Industrial Revolution in the following centuries. A law was passed to restrict the felling of trees in the Weald. Trees here were used to make charcoal for the furnaces, also oak trees were cut and taken to the coast to be used by the Royal Navy for building ships.

In a letter dated 17th August 1693 "John Morfee who served with the Duke of Schomberg in Ireland as conductor to the train of Artillery in Ireland John Morfee gave evidence about Mr Hubbard. Mr Hubbard was ordered to state his account".

The Duke of Schomberg was Frederick Herman 1st Duke of Schomberg, a distinguished general of the 17th century. He was William III chief general in Ireland. He was killed at the Battle of the Boyne in 1690.

Mr Hubbard was William Hubbald, the paymaster of the artillery train in Ireland. It was found there were financial discrepancies in his accounts when returning from Ireland. After his death William Hubbald had his estates seized in Surrey and sold to repay debt to the crown.

John Morfee served in Ireland with William III army might be the reason for some Morphews being called Morphey or Murphey, such as many of those who went to the Colonies in America during the 17th century. Williams's army composed of many Dutch soldiers commanded by Dutch Generals, with this back ground and being in Ireland as well it could be possible that Morfee and later Morphew became corrupt as Murphey in Britain and also the British colonies in America.

We find numerous records of Morphews in Surrey, Sussex and Suffolk

In Surrey Morphews moved away from Bletchingley to Merstham. This is still in the Iron Stone and Green Stone, also Fullers Earth region of the South Downs.

In Sussex Morphews cluster close to where the Maufes had land and property at Chiddingley and Ripe. Also where there were furnaces in Burwash, Mayfield, Hoathly and Rotherfield.

In Suffolk the Morphews concentrated around Hoxne. There are records of Morfeys and Morphew's as the early settlers in the American colony of Virginia.

Surrey Morphews

William Morphewe: 1600 burial Bletchingley.
John Morphewe: 1606 baptised at Bletchingley
John Morfeive (Morfeiue): of Merstham had three children.
John Morphe, Thomas Morfee (Morphew) born 1607

at Merstham, he married Joane and Anne Mafee (Morfee) born in 1600 and died in 1600 at Gatton.
Henrye Morphewe, 1610/11 baptised, Bletchingley.
Nicholas Morphey: marryed Mary Persivall 1612 Merstham.
Elizabeth Morphew, 1612/13 baptised, Bletchingley.
Margaret Morphew: born 1614 Merstham, parents Nicholas and Mary Morphewe.
Dorryty Morphew, 1615 baptised, Bletchingley.
Joane Morphew: born 1616, parent Nicholas and Mary Morfewe.
George Morphew, 1617/18 baptised, Bletchingley.
Richard Mophy (Morphy): the sonne of Nicholas Morphy baptised ye 9 Apr 1620. Spelling from the original parish record, Mophy for Richard but father spelt differently.
Richard Morphye: buried 15th April 1620, sonne of Nicholas Morphye.

In September 1620 a warrant was issued to Thomas Bonde, one of the messengers of his Majesty's Chamber, to bring before the Privy Council workers who had defected from the Banqueting House at Whitehall. The two plasterers named in the bond were John Morphew (Murphy) and Henry Chippinge. Summerson surmised that these defectors were journeymen, but while this was true of Chippinge, who had completed his apprenticeship only the year before, Murphy was already a householder with an apprentice of his own. Presumably these two plasterers were typical of the ambitious young men who resented the interruption of their own careers for the sake of a royal building project. This was a common problem where artisans and skilled laborers were requested to attend at the Kings request. Some absconded due to lack of pay and length of time required to attend.

Thomas Morphee: born in 1620 at Merstham, he married Elizabeth at Merstham. Elizabeth Morphew born 1633 at Merstham.
Thomas Morphew had three children.
Anna Morphew: born 1621 Merstham, parent Nicholas Morphew.
Mary Morphie: Wife of Nicholas Morphie (Morphew) buried 1624, Merstham.
John Morfee (Morfew): born 1644, place unknown.
Johannes Morphee: born in 1645 at Merstham. Parents Thomas and Elizabeth Morphee. This entry in the Merstham parish is written in Latin.
Richard Morphew: born in 1655 at Merstham he died in 1723. Parent Thomas Morphew. Richard Morphew had four children.
Margaret Morphew: 1663 married Walsingham Thorneton at Merstham.
Elizabeth Morphew: born 1663 Merstham, parents Thomas and Joane Morphew.
Elizabeth Morfew: born 1669, Kingston, (Kingston upton Thames). *All saints kingstn*
Jane Morphew: either born or married 1674 at Merstham she married John Coxe.
James Morfew: born 1676, place unknown.-
Sarah Morfew: born 1682 Kingston, (Kingston upon Thames). *All saints - kingstn.*
Ann Morphew: born in 1686 at Merstham.
Richard Morphew: born in 1686 Merstham. Parents, Richard and Elizabeth Morphew.
John Morphew: born in 1688 at Merstham. . Parents, Richard and Elizabeth Morphew.

Elizabeth Morphew: born in 1695 at Merstham. Parent Richard Morphew.
James Morfew: born 1696 Kingston, Kingston upon Thames.

Sussex Morphews
John Morphew: born 1601 at Mayfield. Parents William Morphew
Margaret Morphew: born 1610 at Mayfield
William Morphew: born 1612 at Mayfield
John Morfey: born in 1615 at Framfield
Margaret Morfey: born in 1615 at Framfield
Alyce Morphew: born 1616 at Mayfield
William Mayfield: of Lewes, Will, 1619
Elizabeth Morphew: born in 1620 at Framfield
John Morphew: born in 1620 at Buxted.
Edward Morphewe: 1625 married in Burwash.
Mary Morphee: born 1625 Burwash.
Thomas Morphewe: burial 1628, Burwash.
Edward Morphewe: 1629 baptised Burwash.
Margaret Morphew, 1632 baptised, Burwash.
Mary Morfey: born in 1635 at Buxted
Thomas Morfey: born in 1635 at Newick.
Anne Morphew, 1635/36 baptised, Burwash.
Thomas Morfey: 1635 married Mary Snat at Newick.
Margaret Morphewe: born in 1637 at Buxted; parents John Morfey and Margaret Morfey
Elizabeth Morphew, 1637/38 baptised, Burwash.
Elizabeth Morphewe: born in 1638 at Buxted; parents John Morfey and Margaret Morfey.
Joane Morphew, 1639/40 baptised, Burwash.
Thomas Morphew: born in 1640 at Etchingham.

Alice Morphew, 1642 baptised, Burwash.
William Morphew: born in 1655 at Buxted.
Thomas Morphew, 1659 Baptised, Burwash.
Thomas Morphew: born in 1661 at Buxted; parents Thomas Morfey and Mary Morfey.
Mary Morphee: born in 1663 at Rotherfield, parents Thomas and Mary Morfey
John Morphew: born in 1664 at Burwash, parents Thomas and Mary Morphew, died in 1664 at Burwash
Samuel Morphew: born in 1665 at Burwash, parents Thomas and Mary Morphew.
John Morphew: born in 1666 at Buxted.
Gulielmus Morphew, 1670 baptised, Burwash.
William Morphew: born in 1670 at Burwash, parents Thomas and Mary Morphew.
Joseph Morphew: born in 1673 at Burwash, parents Thomas and Mary Morphew., died 1744.
Elizabeth Morphew: born in 1675 at Fletching.
John Morphew: born in 1675 at Rotherfield, parents John and Elizabeth Morphew
Mary Morphew: born in 1675 at Rotherfield
Hannah Morphew: born 1676 at Bodiam
John Morphew: born in 1695 at Rotherfield
Mary/Maria Morphew: born in 1696 at Burwash.
Mary Morphew: born in 1697 at Rotherfield.
Elizabeth Morphew, 1697/98 baptised, Burwash.

Middlesex (London) Morphews
Stephen Morphewe: 1666, married Margaret Warden Knightsbridge.
Thomas Morfey: 1669

Daniel Morphe: buried in 1671

Richard Morfey: married Sarah Bushell in 1675
Elizabeth Morfey: married George Cottey in 1673
Thomas Morphey: married Margaret Laurence in 1679

Shropshire Morphews
Andrew Morphe: married Sarah Bromly in 1626

Essex Morphews
John Morphewe: 1611, record at Dedham.
John Morffe, Morfee: will, 1693 Colchester.

Norfolk Morphews
Rebecca Morphew, 1611 baptised, Pulham St. Mary
John Morphewe: 1613 baptism, Dickleburh with Langmere.
Margareta Morphew, 1613/14 baptised, Tibenham.
John Morphewe: 1615 burial, Dickleburgh with Langmere.
Elizabeth Morphew, 1615 baptised, Pulham St. Mary.
Thomas Morphew, 1615 baptised, Pulham St. Mary.
Ane (Ann) Morphewe: 1616 Baptism Dickleburgh with Langmere.
Johanes Morphew, 1617 baptised, Tibenham.
Rebecca Morphew, 1618 baptised, Pulham St. Mary.
Richard Morphewe: 1619 baptised at Dickleburgh with Langmere.
Thomas Morphew, 1620 baptised, PulhamSt. Mary.
Thomas Morphewe: 1621 baptised Dickleburgh with Langmere.
John Morphew, 1622 baptised, Thorpe Abbotts.

Anna Morphew, 1622 baptised, Tibenham.

Susan Morphewe: 1624 baptised at Dickleburgh with Langmere.
Marie Morphewe: 1634 married at Rushall.
Rebecca Morphewe: 1637 recorded at Starston.
Maria Morphew, 1641 baptised, Tibenham.
Johannis Morphew, 1643 baptised, Tibenham.
Margaretta Morphew, 1643 baptised, Tibenham.
Edward Morphew, 1643 baptised, Rushall.
John Morphew, 1645 baptised, Dickleburgh.
Johannes Morphew, 1646 baptised, Tibenham.
John Morphew, 1646/47 baptised, Dickleburgh.
Josephus Morphew, 1648 baptised, Tibenham.
Susan Morphew, 1649 baptised, Dickleburgh.
Ann Morphew, 1650/51 baptised, Dickleburgh.
Nathaniel Morphew, 1651/52 baptised, Dickleburgh.
Susan Morphew, 1653/54 baptised, Dickleburgh.
Thomas Morphew, 1656/57 baptised, Dickleburgh.
Robert Morphew, 1661 baptised, Dickleburgh.
Thomas Morphew, 1662 baptised, Rushall.
John Morphew, 1666/67 baptised, Denton.
Elizabeth Morphew, 1669 baptised, Denton.
Isaac Morphew, 1670/71 baptised, Denton.
William Morphew, 1670/71 baptised, Denton.
Jam: Morphew, 1672 baptised, Denton.
Joanna Morphew, 1672 baptised, Thorpe Abbotts.
Mary Morphew, 1674 baptised, Aslacton.
Thomas Morphew, 1675/76 baptised, Alsacton.
Richard Morphew, 1676 baptised, Thorpe Abbotts.
Mary Morphew, 1676/77 baptised, Dickleburgh.
Johannis Morphew, 1677 baptised, Tibenham.
James Morphew, 1677 baptised, Denton.

Elizabeth Morphew, 1679 baptised, Aslacton.
Anna Morphew, 1679 baptised, Tibenham.
John Morphew, 1680 baptised, Dickleburgh.
Edward Morphew, 1681 baptised, Dickleburgh.
Josophus Morphew, 1682 baptised, Tibenham.
Ruth Morphew, 1682 baptised, Tibenham.
John Morphew, 1682/83 baptised, Thorpe Abbotts.
Samuel Morphew, 1685 baptised, Dickleburgh.
Jana Morphew, 1685 baptised, Tibenham.
John Morphew, 1687 baptised, Dickleburgh.
Thomas Morphew, 1687 baptised, Tibenham.
Josephus Morphew, 1689 baptised, Tibenham.
William Morphew, 1690 baptised, Dickleburgh.
Johannis Morphew, 1690 baptised, Tibenham.
Edward Morphew, 1690/91 baptised, Thorpe Abbotts.
Elizabeth Morphew, 1691 baptised, Dickleburgh.
Richard Morphew, 1696 baptised, Thorpe Abbotts.
Mary Morphew, 1696/97 baptised, Dickleburgh.

Suffolk Morphews
Margaret Morphew, 1604 baptised, Lowestoft.
Margaret Morphewe: married William Storer in 1607at Metfield.
Jedion Morphewe: married Elizabeth Payne in 1629 at Hoxne.
Robert Morphew: married Salome Clark in 1634 at Hoxne.
Mary Morphew, 1637 baptised, Bury St. Edmunds.
Thomas Morphew, 1639 baptised, Bury st. Edmunds.

William Goodram: married Sarah Morphewe in 1639 at Hoxne.

Grace Morphewe: 1644 married at Lindsey
John Harper married Jane Morphew in 1652 at Hoxne.
Frances Morphew: married Thomas Bungay in 1658 at Hoxne.
William Morphew: married Rebecca White in 1669 at Hoxne.
John Morphew: married Hannah Branch in 1685 at Hoxne
John Morphewe: 1686 marriage, person and place unknown.
Mrs Rebecca Morphew: Mr Thomas Freen of Wilby married in 1692 at Hoxne.

Kent Morphews
Elizabeth Morfey: married George Cottey in 1673
Elizabeth Morphey: of Godstone married Thomas White of Tonbridge in 1675.

Lancashire Morphews
James Morfey: married Elizabeth Mercer of Leverpool (Liverpool) in 1699.

Gloucestershire Morphews
Richard Murphy: 1682 married Rachel Johns Bristol.

Devon Morphews
Edmund Morphe: baptised, termed as an Irishman in 1621

Somerset Morphews
Christiane Marife: buried 1623.

Cornwall Morphews
John Morphewe: Married 1647, St. Gluvias.

America Morphews
In 1607 the British settlement of James Town, Virginia was established at the request of James I, these initial settlers were all males.
Later many of the settlers in Virginia were indentured Servants. They sailed from Briistol and London and their passage was paid for by the Virginia Company. The servants had to pay this fee back in return by working on the land with a supposed promise of land after four or eight years contracted service.
1619 saw the first African slaves arrive in James Town. Slaves had been in the America's for some time in the Spanish colonies
In 1620 a second colony was established at Cape Cod by the Puritans. After that several other colonies were established in Virginia.
Charles I granted for a colonial settlement in the province of Maryland to begin in 1634 which was to be tolerant toward Catholics.
The early settlements economies were based on tobacco. The seeds had been smuggled from the Spanish who held a tobacco monopoly in Europe. They banned any export of tobacco plants under threat of death.
It is estimated between half and two-thirds of the white male and female immigrants in the British colonies, especially Virginia were indentured. By 1620 there was a tobacco boom which created a demand for servants. By 1683 there were 12,000 Indentured Servants in Virginia and made up a sixth of the population.
The intial indentured contract introduced by the Virginia Company in 1609 involved the servants being

transported at the expense of the Virginian Company and the servants worked directly for the company for five years. The conditions were harsh, the labour was

arduous, accommodation and food was lacking. Of the first 102 Pilgrims who landed at Plymouth in 1620 half died in the first winter. Some 40% of the children born in the 17th century did not reach adult hood.
Settlers had to face the prospect of diseases and infection. In 1657 and 1687 there was an out break of Measles which at the time could prove fatal for children. In 1690 there was a out break of Yellow Fever which has been attributed to ships arriving from the Carribean Islands carrying the lavae in their water stores on board.
Some servants ran away to live with the indiginuous population (Indians). Any absconders who were captured faced severe punishment, either being hung, burnt to death or shot.
In 1619 the indentured servant's contracts changed. The Virginia Company would pay the passage then rent the servant to a tobacco planter for a year. This was to ensure the servant had accommodation and would learn to settle in. The conditions were equally harsh and the mortality rate was high.
In 1620 the contracts were changed again. The Virgina Company still paid for the passage of the individual but the planters could buy the servant. This method lasted in to the 18th century.
Some servants volunteered to be transported to Virginia but they tended not to have a contract and were taken advantage of. They tended to be teenagers such as Joan Morfew who was 15 years of age.
A few of the servants that arrived in Virginia were kidnapped, presumably to meet the high demand for labour in the tobacco plantations.

By 1624 the Virginia Company ceased trading and Virginia was made a royal colony by James I.

By the turn of the century there were landless individuals who would come aboard the ships and buy up several servants and then drive them across the country like sheep, selling them as they went.

The servants had few rights. They could not marry without the permission of their master. If they did marry they could be sentenced by the court for up to twenty lashes on a bare back. If they married clandestinely and had children the children were indentured until the age of twenty one.

Sex between servants was forbidden. A court ruling in 1666 sentenced 'Jane Dolis, a servant for fornicating to receive twenty lashes until her back bled or pay 500lb of tobacco.

As well as Endentured Servants there were mail order brides. This came about to ensure that the immigrated males did not return to England having made their fortune or the Colonies would be lost.

Women were enticed to sail to the American colonies with new clothes and money. They were cared for until they managed to marry one of the male colonials. The women recruited to the American colonies were not forced to marry and could only marry men who had some standing. Equally the brides once married had some standing on colonial society.

By 1629 there were several colonies in what was called New England. Each colony had its own governor.

The first Africans to arrive in Virginia were treated the same as the white indentured servants and were also referred to as servants. In 1661 these rules changed when the 'Slave Law' was passed.

1639 Michaell [sic] Morphew was sponsored by Richard Preston. He arrived in Upper New Norfolk. A court record dated between 1640-1645 in Northumberland shows a James Morphew who was an

Overseer to Mr John Wilkins 'hath most inhumanly beate and abused James Williams, an apprentice'. Early records show a Michael Morphew landed in Virgina in 1641.
1650 Thomas Malfe and amd William Malfe were sponsored by Richard Axom and Thomas Godwin.
1652 James Morphew, a servant or overseer to William Stone esq.. James neglected to plant the tobacco seed due to drink.

1664 a Patrick Morphew is recorded in Northumberland County, Virginia. Patrick Morphew and John Taylor were servants to Christopher Garlington for 5 years. Patrick Morphew was in court the same year for killing wild pigs for his wife.
James Morphew was transported to Maryland in 1648, he was a servant at St. Marys Hundred. He became an Overseer. Another record shows a Mary Morfey being sponsored by William Gooch to sail with others to Virginia in 1650. In the Sussex list above is a Mary Morfey born in 1635 at Buxted. William Gooch sponsored 6 others, paying their passage for land in return.
Westmoreland was established in 1653 after separating from Northumberland County and named 'English County of Westmoreland'.

1661 Talbot County Court, Maryland. Mary Benan, servant to James Murphew ran away but her master forgave her. The court ordered Mary Benan to serve her master, James Murphew.

A Cornelius Morphew in Westmoreland, Virginia is recorded in 1667 being sold land by John Payne.

There are various records of Cornelius Morphew and Murfee in Westmoreland County between1668 to 1694. They involve in court cases and accusations of theft. 1669 Mary Morphew was born, her parents were Richard and Issabell Morphew.

A record shows Elinor Morphew born in 1672. The parents were Richard Morphew and Izabel Morphew. In 1675 Anne Arundel County Patrick Morphew is in debt to to Thomas Urner and again in debt in 1677 1663, Talbot County Court, James Murphew brought his servant, Natli who was ordred to serve six years. There are several other records of James Murphy,

Murphie, Morphey and Murphew. The last record is of his last will and testament in 1699.
In 1677 Richard Morphew was born, his parents were Richard and Izabel Morphew. That same year Izabel Morphew died.
1679 in Westmorland County Captain John Lord High Sheriff arrested Andrew and at the Suite of Mr. Robert Vaulx, attorney of Step, Morphew for 920 pounds of tobacco.

Record dated 1687 in Westmoreland County, 'up on sufficient proof there is due to John Minor 300 acres of land for the transportation of the after named persons in to the colony', the list included Margaret Murfew.
In 1695 a Bryan Morphew and Edward Morphew is recorded being in Virginia.

In 1697 Mary Morphew, a servant to Peter Starkey died in York County.
Maryland record dated 1696 shows Alexander Lumbley lodged a complaint against Patrick Morphew of Baltimore County.

1699 Joane Morfew, 15 years old was a servant to Nicholas Edwards in Northumberland County. She was ordered to serve her master by the courts.

18th Century

The 18th century saw several attempts to compile dictionaries but they had differences in the spelling of some words. Samuel Johnson published his own dictionary which became recognised as the reference for the correct spelling at the time.

At the start of the 18th century the iron industry in the Weald of Sussex and Kent supplied cannons for the Royal Navy, Army and merchant ships. They were also manufactured for the East India Company. The cannons exported abroad caused concern, it allowed Britians enemy to have access to these well made cannons.

Morphews are recorded in the villages where the foundries were producing and manufacturing the iron and cannons.

These villages were within a small area of the Weald just twenty miles from east to west and ten miles north to south. Several foundaries were just a few miles apart not far from the original land that the Maufe's had at Chiddlingly, Hoathley and Chalvington.

In 1702 a Morphew, (Morphen) is recorded as a surveyor for Houses and Windows duties (taxes).
In Norfolk, 1711 Francis Morphew is a receiver of taxes.
There are several records for a Thomas Morphew who was Marshal of the 1st and 2nd Guards. He was mentioned in a report by Sir Christopher Wren, the architect of St. Pauls Cathedral in London.

"A report by Sir Christopher Wren, Officers of the Works, on the said Morphew's disbursements, detailed, in repairing and keeping in order her Majesty's Marshalsea in the Savoy in 1707, 1708 and 1709.

The first two items were for the benefit of the edifice and reasonable to be made in case the prison had not been there. The account reported on by the Officers of the Works is as follows".
Anne Stuart was crowned Queen of England after James II was deposed.
On 19th February 1711 Thomas Morphew (Marshall to the 1st and 2nd Regiments for Foot Guards) reported from the Officers of the works concerning his petition for repairs to the marshal prison in the Savoy and order it to be read when Mr Howe, paymaster of the Guards and garrisons is present. Also in 1711 Thomas Morphew declared monies to pay for coal, etc for the prison in the Savoy, and for the accommodation of the soldiers and the recruites.
A letter was written to the Secretary at War states "Thomas Morphew, Marshal to the First and Second Regiments of Foot Guards, has exhibited his bill of disbursements for repairing and fitting up the prison in the Savoy and also for necessaries for the recruits secured there in 1707–9. My Lord Treasurer has ordered the charge for said repairs to be taken into the debt of the Office of Works, the same being an edifice belonging to her Majesty. The Paymaster General of Guards and Garrisons proposes meeting the charge of said necessaries out of Contingencies, being £185 5s. 6d. Please obtain a royal warrant for same accordingly".
1714 Anne died at Kennsington Palace. George I succeeded her.

A Lease and release document dated 1722 notes Thomas Morphew at Tandridge, a yeoman and his eldest son George of Richmond.
"1722 'Lease and release by Thomas Morphew, a Yeoman of Tandridge and George Morphew his eldest son of Richmond, paintstainer to William Green the younger of Limpsfield, Yeoman, of Messauge in Tandridge wherein Thomas Morphew now dwells".
1727 George I died at Osnabruk in Germany. He was succeeded by George II

A Chelsea work house recorded a James Morphew who died in 1736 referring to him as, 'a poor stranger of the work house'.
There is a 1736 record of a Thomas Morphey or Morphew esquire living at Coleherne House in Little Chelsea. Coleherne House was a mansion with 3 acres and garden on the Fulham road. To the east were 8 villa's or cottages.
Looking at previous records This Thomas Morphew could be the one born in1661 at Buxted.
Little Chelsea in the 18th century was an exclusive area on the edge of London. Thomas Morgan owned the house at the time and paid the rates. The occupancy changed in 1739. This shows how Morphews were at the extremes of the social ladder.

The 18th century was a turbulent time for Britain. Britain was involved in the War of Spanish Succession at the start of the century. Britain supported Prussia in the Silesian War in 1740 and Seven Years War of 1756 to 1763. There were wars in the colonies especially in America and also India.
A document dated 1763 mentioning Thomas Morphew dwelling in Tandridge.

Britain having established further colonies in America was to loose them in the American War of Independence, (American Revolutionary War) in 1783. It was a time of exploration where Britain was to dominate the high sea's most notably Captain James

Cook who sailed around the world and claimed New Zealand, Australia, Hawaii amongst other dominions for Britain.
Later Britain and its colonies were to be threatened by the French Revolution and the wars that followed in to the 19th Century. The need for cannons and cannon-

balls on ships and for the army was more vital than ever with the defence of the young developing empire. By the mid 1700s blast furnaces in the Weald of Sussex and Kent were starting to go out of business. Production was being moved to the north where there was an abundance of coal that burned at a higher temperature than charcoal. Those who had relied on the iron industry for employment, of which there were many had to find alternative employment. The landed gentry who had leased their land to the foundries and furnace masters also lost income.

William III died at Kensington Palace and succeeded by Anne Queen of Great Britain (England, Scotland, Ireland and Wales).
Anne died in 1714 at Kensington Palace, succeeded by George I.
George I died in 1727 at Schloss Osnabruck, Osnabruck, George II succeeded him.

In 1747 the British Government introduced the window tax. There are records of Morphews in Sussex having to pay window tax. William Morphey at Battle, Thomas Morphew of Peasmarsh, William Morfee at Burwash, George Morphew at Fletching and John Morphew of Bexhill. It would appear that some Morphew's made a good living, possibly out of the iron industry of the Weald.

George II died in 1760 at Kensington Palace and was succeeded by George III.

Surrey Morphews and Morffews

Ann Morphew: born about 1700, place unknown
Gulielmus Morphew, 1700 baptised, Burwash.
Thomas Morphew, 1710 listed in the Poll of the Knights of the Shire. Thomas Morphew lived in Tandridge. The poll was of the free holders of the parish shires taken at Guildford.
Elizabeth Morphew : born 1711 at Merstham parents Richard and Anne Morphew.
Anne Morphew : born 1714, Merstham.
parents Richard and Anne Morphew.
Jane Morphew: born 1716 Merstham. Parents Richard and Anne Morphew.
Richard Morphew: born 1718 at Merstham, married Margaret. Parents Richard and Anne Morphew.
Jane Morphew: born 1718 at Gatton, married Richard Rofley in 1733, parents Richard and Anne Morphew.
John Morphew: born 1721 at Merstham.
parents Richard and Anne Morphew.
Richard Morphew: did 1725 Merstham.
James Morphew: born 1726, a bastard. Parent Anne Morphew

James Morphew: born 1728 Merstham. Married Priscilla Doily. Died 1801
Sarah Morphew, 1737 baptised, Richmond.
Anne Morphew: born 1749 Merstham, parents Richard and Margaret Morphew.
Mary Morphew, 1751 baptised, Merstham.

Mary Morphew: born 1752 Merstham, died 1804 a pauper, parents Richard and Margaret Morphew.
Sarah Morphew: born 1755 Merstham.
Parents, Richard and Margaret Morphew.
James Morphew: married Priscilla Doily 1756 Merstham.
John Morphew: born 1757 Merstham. Parents James and Priscilla Morphew.
John Morphew: buried 1759. Reciding at the poor house.
James Morphew: born 1759 Merstham died 1762. Parents James and Priscilla Morphew.
Richard Morphew: born 1761, Merstham.
Thomas Morphew: born 1762 Ham, parents James and Priscilla Morphew. Married Hannah Percey parents Richard and Margaret Morphew
Anne Morphew: born 1763, place unkown parents Richard and Margaret Morphew.
John Morphew: born 1767 place unknown parents Richard and Margaret Morphew
James Morphew: born 1757 place unknown, died 1801. parent Ann Morphew (barstadised) Married Priscilla Doily 1756.
John Morphew: born 1757 place unknown died 1759. Parents James and Priscilla Morphew.
parents James and Priscilla Morphew.
Martha Morphew: born 1760 Merstham parents James and Priscilla Morphew.

Richard Morphew: born 1761 Merstham, parents James and Priscilla Morphew.
Thomas Morphew: born 1762 Merstham died 1846. Married Hannah Percy at Woking in 1788. Parents James and Priscilla Morphew.

James Morphew: died 1762 Merstham. Parent's James and Priscilla Morphew.
Anne Morphew: born 1763 Merstham. Parent's Richard and Margaret Morphew.
Priscilla Morphew: born 1764 Merstham parents James and Priscilla Morphew.
John Morphew: born 1766 Merstham, parents James and Priscilla Morphew
William Morphew: born 1766 place unkown parents James and Priscilla Morphew.
Richard Morphew, 1766 baptised, Betchworth.
John Morphew: born 1767 Merstham. Parents Richard and Margaret Morphew.
Robert Morphew: born 1769 place unkown parents James and Priscilla Morphew
Mersey Morphew: born 1771 place unkown parents James and Priscilla Morphew.
Anne Morphew: married William Toms in 1772, Merstham.
Benjamin Morphew: born 1774 place unkown parents James and Priscilla Morphew.
James: Record 1776, natural son of John Dod and Mary Morphew.
Edward Morphew, 1776 baptised, Betchworth.
Morphew: 1777 record in Merstham parish as a bastard. Maybe James the natural son of John Dod and Mary Morphew.

Thomas Morffew: born 1780, the earliest recording of the name Morffew.

Sarah Morphew: married Francis Botton in 1781 at Merstham.

Richard Morphew: entry in Merstham parish record in 1785.

John Morphew: died 1786 at Merstham.

Thomas Morffew: born 1782 place unknown, died 1807, an apprentice.

Richard Morffew: born 1790 place unknown, married Harriet Bowbrick. parents Thomas and Hannah Morphew

William James Morffew: born 1791 place unknown, married Elizabeth. Parents Thomas and Hannah Morphew.

Thomas Morffew: born 1794 Kingston upon Thames, married Sarah Collins. Later married Elizabeth Lee

Henry Morffew: born 1795 Kingston upon Thames, a shoe maker, married Sarah Parrott in 1817 at Walton on Thames, parents Thomas and Hannah Morphew. 1871 census at Kingston upton Thames

Robert Wade Morffew: born 1797 place unknown died 1798, parents Thomas and Hannah Morphew.

Hannah Morffew: born 1799 at Kingston upon Thames, married John Duffell, parents Thomas and Hannah Morphew.

Sussex Morphews and Morpheys

William Morphew: born 1700 at Burwash

Thomas Morphew: born 1702 at Rotherfield, parents John and Elizabeth Morphew.

Sarah Morphew: born 1704 at Burwash

Mary Morphew: born 1705 place unknown

Joseph Morphew: born 1706 at Burwash, parents Joseph and Elizabeth Morphew
Thomas Morphew: born 1709 at Burwash, parents Joseph and Mary (Wyatt) Morphew
William Morphew: born 1712 at Fletching
Maria Morphew: born 1713 at Burwash
Elizabeth Morphew: born 1714 at Fletching
George Morphew: born 1717 at Fletching, parents William – a glover and Rachel Morfey
Sarah Morphew: born 1717 at Fletching
John Morphew : born 1718 at Fletching
William Morphey: born 1720 Chiddingly
John Morphew : born 1722 at Fletching.
Mary Morphew: born 1727 at Burwash
Sarah Morphew: born 1729 at Burwash
Thomas Morphey: born 1731 at Warbletoon
William Morphew: born 1732 at Burwash
Sarah Morfey: born 1732 at Warbleton
Mary Morfee: born 1735 at Burwash
John Morphew: born 1737 at Burwash
Elizabeth Morphew: born 1740 at Burwash
Thomas Morphew, 1740 baptised, Sedlescombe.
Mary Morphew, 1741 baptised, Sedlescombe.
Eleanor Morphew: born 1742 at Burwash
John Morphey: born 1742 at Burwash.
John Morphew (Morphey): born 1742 East Grinstead. Parents William and Mary Morphew (Morphey).
Amelia Vinal Morphew: born 1744 at Fletching.
William Morphew, 1744 baptised, Sedlescombe.
Zabulan Morphew, 1744 baptised, Hastings.
John Morphew, born 1745 at Burwash
Margaret Morphey: born 1744/45 at East Grinstead. Parents William and Mary Morphey

John Morphew, 1745 baptised, Fletching.
Elizabeth Morphew, 1746/47 baptised, Sedlescombe.
William Morphey: born 1747 at East Grinstead.

Sarah Morphew, 1750 baptised, Sedlescombe.
George Morphew: born 1751 at East Grinstead, parents William and Mary (Cripps) Morphey.
Thomas Morphew, 1752 baptised, Sedlescombe.
Robert Morphew: born 1754 at East Grinstead
Frances Morphew: born 1755 at Burwash
Rachael Morphew: born 1757 East Grinstead.
Ann Morphew, 1758 baptised, Sedlescombe.
Robert Morphew: born 1760 at East Grinstead
Christopher Morphew: born 1762 at East Grinstead, parents William and Mary Morphey, Christopher was a weaver.
Cripps Morphew: born 1765 East Grinstead, parents William Morphey, Cripps was a flax draper.
Fanny Morphew: born 1765 Burwash.
William Morphew, 1767 baptised, Sedlescombe.
Stephen Morphew, 1770 baptised, Sedlescombe
William and Mary Morphew; born 1772, William married Mildred Cook, a farmer.
Mary Morphew, 1775 baptised, Sedlescombe
Anne Morphey: born 1776 at Fletching
Thomas Morphey: born 1778 at Fletching
John Cripps Morphew: born 1779 at Hartfield.
Winny Morphew, 1779 baptised, Sedlescombe.
Mary Allen Morphew: born 1782 at Hartfield
Harriott Morphew: born 1785 at East Grinstead
James Morphew: born 1787 at Burwash
Keziah Morphew: born 1787 at Burwash, parents John and Sarah Morphew.

Elizabeth Morphew: born 1787 at Hartfield.
George Morphew: born 1788 East Grinstead, parents Robert and Elizabeth Morphew.

Keziah/Heziah Morphew: born 1789 at Burwash, parent Charlotte.
George Morphew: born 1790 at East Grinstead
Elizabeth Morphew: born 1790 at East Grinstead
Robert Cripps Morphew: born 1793 at Hartfield
Elizabeth Morphew: born 1794 at Frant
Sarah Cripps Morphew: born 1795 at East Grinstead
Harriet Morphew: born 1796 at Frant
Mary Morphew: born 1796 at East Grinstead
William Thomas Morphew: born 1796 at Hartfield, parents William and Mildred Morphew, William was a farmer, died 1837 at Hartfield.
John Morphew: born 1799 at East Grinstead

Shropshire Morphews
John Morphew married Elizabeth Rogers in 1736 at Wollen
Rachel Morphey: died 1741 at Wollen
Elizabeth Morphey: baptised 1741 at Wollen
An infant was found at house at the house of Thomas Tyther in 1744. The infant was baptised John Morff at Wollen. He died the same year at Wollen.

Kent Morphews
Elizabeth Morphew, 1700 baptised, Northfleet.
Martha Morphew, 1725 baptised, Lewisham.
Geoffrey/Jeffery Morphew, 1729 baptised, Lewisham.

Mary Morphew, 1730 baptised, Lewisham.
William Morphew, 1732 baptised, Lewisham.
Richard Morphew, 1735/37 baptised, Lewisham.

Cheshire Morphews (Morfe)
Luke Morfe dies 1710

Lancashire Morphews
Mary Morphew, 1710 baptised, Liverpool.

London and Middlesex Morphews
Martha Morphey married Anthony Beaumont in 1700.
John Morphew In the early 1700s had a small publishing business near Stationers Hall. He was associated with significant literary and political publications. At one point publishing for both the Whig and Tory factions, later becoming more associated with the Tories. He died in 1720.
William Morphew, 1721 baptised, Covent Garden.
Elizabeth Morffew: born in 1796 in Holborn, London. She married in 1851 at Kensington.
Elizabeth Morffew: registered as being born in 1798 at Westminster.
Mary Morphew, 1755 baptised, Isleworth.

Suffolk Morphews
John Russell, a Mariner and Sarah Morphew, both of Harwich married 1702.
John Morphew: born about 1759, married Sarah Lee in 1789 at Nedging. Children; William, Joseph, John, James, Elizabeth.

William Morphew: born 1791 at Nedging. Agricultural labourer. Married Muriel Pheobe Squirrel, died 1871 at Nedging.
Mary Morphew: born 1796. Married John Squirrel, died 1833.

Robert Morphew: born 1798 at Nedging. Cordwainer, married Mary Marchant, died 1849

Essex Morphews
Robert Morffe Merchant of Rotterdam, Holland. 1702 his will at Chelmsford.
Robert Morffe Say maker 1713 Colchester will.
Elizabeth Morphew, 1714/15 baptised, Manningtree.
Thomas Morphew, 1735 baptised, Manningtree.
Thomas Morphew, 1745 baptised, Manningtree.
John Morphew, 1746 baptised, Manningtree.
Mary Morphew, 1749 baptised, Manningtree.
John Morphew, 1751 baptised, Manningtree.
Thomas Morphew, 1777 baptised, Manningtree.
Mary Morphew, 1779 baptised, Mistley.
Jane Morphew, 1784 baptised, Mistley.
Sarah Morphew, 1786 baptised, Mistley.
George Morphew, 1793 baptised, Mistley.
Charlotte Morphew, 1793 baptised, Mistley.
Hetty Morphew, 1793 baptised, Mistley.
Daniel Morphew, 1793 baptised, Mistley.

Norfolk Morphews
John Morphew, 1707 baptised, Norwich.
Elizabeth Morphew, 1710 baptised, Dickleburgh.
Elizabeth Morphew, 1711 baptised, Ketteringham.
Elizabeth Morphew, 1711/12 baptised, Shimpling.

James Morphew, 1712 baptised, Norwich.
Joseph Morphew, 1712 baptised, Ketteringham.
Edward Morphew, 1713/14 baptised, Shimpling.
Ruth Morphew, 1715 baptised, Ketteringham.
John Morphew, 1716 baptised, Shimpling.
John Morphew, 1716 baptised, Yelverton.
Anne Morphew, 1718 baptised, Shimpling.
Edward Morphew, 1718 baptised, Thorpe Abbotts.
Mary Morphew, 1720 baptised, Shimpling.
Edward Morphew, 1721 baptised, Thorpe Abbotts.
James Morphew, 1721 baptised, Great Yarmouth.
Samuel Morphew, 1724/25 baptised, Dickleburgh.
Mary Morphew, 1728 baptised, Norwich.
Wigget Morphew, 1735 baptised, Norwich.
James Morphew, 1736 baptised, Norwich.
John Morphew, 1737 baptised, Brockdish.
James Morphew, 1737/38 baptised, Norwich.
Benjamin Morphew, 1738/39 baptised, Norwich.
Mary Morphew, 1739 baptised, Earsham.
John Morphew, 1740/41 baptised, Earsham.
Elizabeth Morphew, 1741 baptised, Carleton.
Mary Wiggett Morphew, 1741 baptised, Norwich.
Mary Morphew, 1742/43 baptised, Carleton.
Jemima Morphew, 1745 baptised, Diss.
John Morphew, 1745 baptised, Carleton.
Susanna Morphew, 1747 baptised, Diss.
Mary Morphew, 1747/48 baptised, Norwich.
Elizabeth Morphew, 1748/49 baptised, Diss.
Elizabeth Morphew, 1751 baptised, Norwich.
John Morphew, 1752 baptised, Norwich.
Hannah Morphew, 1753 baptised, Diss.
Edward Morphew, 1754 baptised, Diss.
Susan Morphew, 1756 baptised, Norwich.

Mary Morphew, 1756 baptised Diss.
Hannah Morphew, 1757 baptised, Diss.
Abigail Morphew, 1759 baptised, Diss.
Hannah Morphew, 1761 baptised, Babngley.
Charlotte Morphew, 1761 baptised Diss.
Edward Morphew, 1765 baptised, Diss.
Sarah Morphew, 1767 baptised, Diss.
John Morphew: 1768 Electoral Register at Little Ellingham.
Mary Morphew, 1773 baptised, Great Yarmouth.
William Morphew, 1773 baptised, Redenhall.
Joseph Briggs Morphew, 1781 baptised, Easton.
Samuel Morphew, 1783 baptised, Foxley.
Susanna Morphew, 1786 baptised, Worthing.
Thomas Morphew, 1794 baptised, Norwich.
Jane Morphew, 1799 baptised, Norwich
.

Lincolnshire Morphews

Mary Morphew, 1762 baptised, Corby.
Elizabeth Morphew, 1762 baptised, Corby.
Catherine Morphew, 1762 baptised, Corby

Northumberland Morphews

Unknown Morphew, 1712/13 baptised, Hexham.

Cornwall Morphews

Moses Morphew, 1726 baptised, Falmouth.

Huntingdonshire Morphews

Mary Morphew, 1798 baptised, Yaxley.

American Morphews

By the turn of the century the British colonies in Virginia, Maryland, Northumberland and Westmoreland were fully established.

Indentured Servants were still being transported to Virginia as demand for tobacco increased in Britain. Mis-spelling of the Morphew name seems to be quite common, just as in Britain.

In the mid 1700s there was the French Indian Wars. These ended in 1764 at the end of the Seven Years War.

The American War of Independence (Revolutionary War) broke out in 1775 and ended in 1783 soon after the British surrender at Yorktown.

Nicholas Murfew: in 1700 of Northumberland County was a servant to Mr Daniel Sivillivant.
John Murphew: married Mary Eliot (Elliot) in 1707 at St. Georges parish church near Perryman, Hartford County. John and mary had five children.
Darcas Murphew: born 1709.
John Murphey (Murffy): born 1710.
Edward Murffy: born 1712.
Cathurinah Morphew: born 1719.
Timothy Morphew: born 1721.
John Murphey (Murfey): died 1729. Last will and testament left to his son John half fifty acres, other half to his son Edward at Murpheys Hazard.
Nicholas Murphy: in 1720 recorded in a court in York County

1708 Major Radham Kenner was given 700 acres for transporting 34 people including jone (Joan) Murphew
Henry Murphew: recorded in Northumberland County in 1713.

Terence Murphew: servant to William Heath.
James Morphew: born England about 1715/1725, died 1783. Married Mary Burk on 9th October 1749, Old Augusta County, Virginia.
Augusta County land entry on September 24th 1753. James Morphew 150 acres between Matthew Black, Cravins and Daniel Loves Meadow.
There are records relating to James and Michael Morphew/Murphy in the mid 1700s when the French Indian War was being waged
Elizabeth Murphew: 1716 in Northumberland County was a servant to William medcalf agreed in court to serve her master for a year after her indentured time expired. This can be construed that Elizabeth had commited a mistermeanor.
Alexander Murphew: 1722 married Ann Darbin in King George County, Virginia.
James Morphew/ Murphey: was a tax runaway in 1750. James Morphew married Betty Chadwich in 1774. Lived in Surry County, North Carolina until 1799, in Wilks County, North Carolina until 1811 and then Peble County, Ohio.
James Morphew II: born 1750 Dublin, Polaski County, Virginia. He died 1812 (another record states 1829) in Guildford County, North Carolina.
Silas Morphew: born 1752 and died 1808. Married Elizabeth England in Chatham County.
Helen Morphew: 1723 married Thomas Williams.
Frances Murphy: born 1725. Parents Alexander and Anne Murphy.

Sarah Murphew: born 1731, parents Alexander and Anne Murphew.

Frances Murfee: in 1731, mentioned in the will of Mark Jones in King George County, 'I give to a little girl by name of Frances Murfee a good feather bed and furniture.
Sarah (Sally) Morphew: born 1754 and died 1840. Sally Married Young Coleman. Coleman family remembered in bible of Minnesota reverend William Morphew.
Land entry January 1754 in Augusta County. Michael Morphew 200 acres on a small branch, west side of dry river in mountain.
James Morphew: a deed for dated 1756. James was written as being of Rowan County in the Province of North Carolina.
Mary Morphew: born 1759 and died 1810. Married Ephriam Norris on 7th April 1792, in Wilkes County.
James Morphew: 1759 tax record in Rowan County, North Carolina.
Anna Morphew: born c. 1760.
Timothy & Elizabeth Murphy: 1760 sold 100 acres for £90 to Aquila Hall in Baltimore County, Maryland.
Naomi Morphew: born 1760 and died 1806. Married Ephriam Johnson in Wilkes County 28th February 1791.
Joseph Murphey/Morphew: 1768 tax record for in Rowan County.
Richard Morphee: 1771 record of in Surry County, North Carolina.
Joseph Morphew: born 1771 in North Carolina, or about 1775/1776. Married Avis Eggers about 1797.

Parents James Morphew and Betty.
19th April 1775 the American War of Independence (American Revolutionary War) broke out. This was to last until 1783 with thirteen colonies revolting, these were North and South Carolina, Georgia, Virginia, Maryland, New Jersey, Pennsylvania, New Hampshire, Maine, Massachusetts, Quebec, New Foundland and Nova Scotia.

James Morphee: 1782 in Surry [sic] County had 300 acres at Waters of Hunting Creek
Record 1783 in Surry County of James Burke Sr. was probated in Surry County mentioning Mary Morphew and Grand Daughter Sarah Morphew. The will does not mention Mary Burke Morphew husband.
1784 James Murphy of Surry County has 200 acres and James Murphee has 300 acres.
1786 in Surry County, North Carolina Silas Murphew, James Murphy had 300 acres. Joseph Murphy has 100 acres.

1789 George Washington took office as President.

1797 John Adams took office as President.

19th Century

At the turn of the century the iron industry in the Weald of Sussex had dwindled to just one furnace at Ashburnham which eventually closed in 1813.
In 1808 a Mr William Banister was imprisoned in the Prison Hulk 'Retribution' moored at Woolwich and then at Sheerness. He wrote home to his wife and children and commented in his letter 'if I get my Liberty I will seek out that Villan [sic] of a morfey that brought me in to this troble [sic] that all their rogery'. A prison hulk was a moored disused naval ship that held prisoners, in many cases before being transported to the colonies. Iron Stone and Green Stone was still being mined in Surrey and used for construction in London.
During the 19th Century the Morffew appears for in further records in Surrey and London. Residing in Ham and Petersham near Kingston upon Thames at first but several moved to Chelsea which was on the outskirts of London at the time. In the Mid 1850s a Morffew family immigrated to Australia and settled in the Melbourne region of Victoria.
At the start of the 19th Century Britain was embroiled in the Napoleonic Wars that raged across Europe and the colonies. Britain also had to contend with fighting America. America launched a number of attacks across the Great Lakes on Canada. This came to a head when Britain sent to Canada a number of veteran troops of the Iberian Peninsula. A hard fought war where the British army, commanded Wellington attacked Spain, assisted by Portugal drove the French back across the Pyrenees.

These British troops were landed on American soil with the intention to stop the Americans attacking Canada by capturing Washington. The British troops did this

and burnt down the capital.
Even though the British suffered considerable losses in this campaign it stopped any further attacks by America. This became known as the War of 1812.
1820 George III died at Windsor Castle, he was succeeded by George IV.
1830 George IV died at Windsor Castle, he was succeeded by William IV.
1837 William IV died at Windsor Castle, he was succeeded by Queen Victoria.
In America the differences over the slaves in the Southern States resulted in the American Civil War that lasted four years, 1861 to 1865. This war proved deadly with the introduction of magazine fed rifles replacing single shot muskets.
A number of British nationals migrated to Canada but found the weather too harsh, they either returned home or migrated South.
In Offham, Kent, England there is a Morphews cottage, Morphew Farm and Morphew Oasts. Oasts or Oast houses were common though out Kent. They were large kilns used for drying hops before being sent to the brewers.
Cripps Morphew was a flax draper. Flax was from the linseed plant was combed and woven in to yarn. This had been used since medieval times to make linen. A draper was a sales merchant.
In the 1840 London Gazette a Benjamin Morphew who was formally living at No45 Titchfield St., Mary le Bone, (Marylebone). He was a carpenter, undertaker and blindmaker. Prior to this he was at No 3 Great Ogle St. Mary le Bone where he was refered to as a carpenter

and journeyman.Both addresses of Middlesex. Benjamin Morphew was incarserated in the debtor prison. Today there is Great Titchfield St. that runs

from Green St. close to the A501down to Oxford Circus market near the A40. Ogle St. is two streets away which run from New Cavendish St. to Foley St. Marlebone was greatly developed in the 18th century with new buildings and roads being constructed to accommodate the traffic coming in to London. Reverend J.C. Morphew was at Crimplesham, West Norfolk in 1864. Here there are memorials to the Creasy Family.

Surrey Morphews

James Morphew: died 1801 Merstham, died of diarrohea.
Mary Morphew: 1804 Merstham record, suddenly becomes a pauper. Born 1752 in Merstham. Died 1804.
Ann Morphew, 1806 baptised, Beddington.
Frances Morphew, 1812 baptised, Merstham, parents Francis William and Ann Morphew
Elizabeth Morphew, 1815 baptised, Merstham..
Henry Morffew: born 1820 Kingston upon Thames. 1841 census at Kingston. Married 1847 at Kennington, Lambeth. 1871 census at Chelsea. Died 1874 at Chelsea.
Sarah Morphew, 1827 baptised, Merstham.
Elizabeth Jane Morphew: born 1838 Bermondsey.
Eliza Phebe Morphew: born 1845 Bermondsey.
Rachel Morphew: born 1847 Wandsworth.
Male Morphew: born 1847 Chertsey.
Jane Standen Morphew: born 1847 Lambeth.

James Robert Morphew: born 1849 Bermondsey.
Henry Morffew: born 1849 Chelsea.
Sarah Ann Morphew: born 1851 Bermondsey.
Isabella Jane Morphew: born 1852 Chertsey.
Menah Elizabeth Morphew: born 1852 Southwark.
William Morphew: born 1853 Newington.
John Morphew: born 1854 Chertsey.
Frederick Charles Morphew: born 1856 Camberwell.
William George Morphew: born 1856 Newington.
Elizabeth Jane Briggs: born 1857 Newington.
Ellen Jane Morphew: born 1857 Newington.
Thomas Briggs Morphew: born 1859 Camberwell.
Arthur James Briggs Morphew: born 1861 Camberwell.
Louisa Alice Morphew: born 1863 Camberwell.
William Wood Morphew: born 1863 Camberwell
Harriet Elizabeth Morphew: born 1865 Camberwell.
Arthur Ermest H. Morphew: born 1867 Lambeth.
Margaret Gertrude Morphew: born 1867 Lambeth.
Fanny Louisa Morphew: born 1868 Wandsworth.
Harry Archery Morphew: born 1868 Wandsworth.
Frances Mary Morphew: born 1868 Wandsworth.
George Edward Morphew: born 1868 Camberwell.
Frederick Arthur W. Morphew: born 1869 Lambeth.
Ethel Mary Morphew: born 1869 Lambeth.
Frederick Charles Morphew: born 1870 Wandsworth.
Ellen Amelia Morphew: born 1870 Wandsworth.
Joseph John B. Morphew: born 1870 Camberwell.
William Charles Morphew: born 1870 Wandsworth.
Lydia Blanche Morphew: born 1871 Lambeth.
George Mark Morphew: born 1871 Wandsworth.
Allan Lachlan Morphew: born 1872 Wandsworth, married Mary Isabelle Nash in 1895. Mary inherited property from her grandparents. A house at 7 Finch Lane London, two houses at Kings Road, Brighton, Sussex. A house in Cobham, Surrey and a house with

garden in Queens Street, Kingston (Kingston upon Thames), Surrey.

Sarah Jane Morphew: born 1872 Camberwell.
Florence Lydia Morphew: born 1872 Wandsworth.
James Charles B. Morphew: born 1873 Camberwell.
Ada Louisa Morphew: born 1873 Lambeth.
Perry Holden Morphew: born 1874 Lambeth.
James Ellen Morphew: born 1874 Wandsworth.
Reginald Morphew: born 1874 Wandsworth. Died 1971. Was an architect and an accomplished artist who's watercolours are held at the Victoria and Albert Museum in London.
Thomas Briggs Morphew: born 1874 Wandsworth.
Walter Charles B Morphew: born 1875 Camberwell.
Thomas Henry Morphew: born 1876 Wandsworth.
Florence Morphew: born 1876 Southwark.
Jeffery Morphew: born 1876 Wandsworth.
Mary Jane J. B. Morphew: born 1876 Camberwell.
Jessie Morphew: born 1877 Wandsworth.
Alice Louisa Morphew: born 1877 Wandsworth.
Charlotte A. Briggs Morphew: born 1878 Camberwell.
Albert Edgar Morphew: born 1878 Lambeth.
Rose Anna Morphew: born 1878 Wandsworth.
Bernard Scott Morphew: born 1878 Southwark.
Charlotte Ada Morphew: born 1878 Camberwell
Charles Henry Morphew: born 1880 Epsom.
Sidney Reece Morphew: born 1880 Southwark.
Harold Morphew: born 1880 Wandsworth.
Henry Edward G. K. Morphew: born 1880 Southwark. Military record: service number 3487, Sergeant in 1914 Royal Fusiliers.
Robert Ernest Morphew: born 1882 Wandsworth.
Edward Morphew: born 1883 Lambeth.
Elizabeth Louisa Morphew: born 1884 Camberwell.

Rowland Owen Morphew: born 1884 Southwark.
Edwin Frank Morphew: born 1884 Wandsworth.

Edwin James Morphew: born 1885 Wandsworth.
William James A Morphew: born 1886 Camberwell.
Marion Evelyn Morphew: born 1887 Southwark.
Mary Louisa E Morphew: born 1888 Wandsworth.
Alice Morphew: born 1889 Camberwell.
Florence Elizabeth Morphew: born 1894 Camberwell.
Emily Myra Morphew: born 1895 Lambeth.
Ernest Morphew: born 1886 Lambeth.
James Francis W. Morphew: born 1886 Wandsworth.
William Morphew: born 1890 Lambeth.
Richard Henry Morphew: born 1891 Wandsworth.
Lydia Maud Morphew: born 1893 Lambeth.
William George Morphew: born 1893 Wandsworth.
Willie Morphew: born 1893 Richmond
Henry Morphew: born 1895 Wandsworth.
Alice Gray Morphew: born 1896 Wandsworth.
Joseph John Morphew: born 1896 Camberwell.
Edith Florence Morphew: born 1896 Lambeth.
Hilda Ellen Morphew: born 1897 Lambeth.
Alfred William Morphew: born 1897 Camberwell.
Lily Violet Morphew: born 1897 Camberwell.
Henry Charles Morphew: born 1898 Wandsworth.
John Edward Morphew: born 1898 Croydon.
Florence Elizabeth Morphew: born 1899 Camberwell.
Lion Elvin K. Morphew: born 1899 Croydon.

Sussex Morphews and Morpheys

Joan Morphew: born 1800, Frant, parents William Morphew a farmer & Mildred Morphew a cook.
Susan Morphew: born 1800 Withyham, died 1805.

Elizabeth Morphew: born 1802 East Grinstead, parents Cripps Morphew a Flax Draper & Ann Morphew.

William Morphew: born 1804 East Grinstead, parents Cripps Morphew a flax daper & Ann Morphew.
George Morphew: born 1804 Rotherfield a Shop keeper and farmer, parents William Morphew farmer & Mildred Morphew.
Thomas Mills Morphew: born 1805 Rotherfield, parents William Morphew a farmer & Mildred Morphew a cook.
 Mary Ann Morphew: born 1805, parent John Morphew a farmer.
Rachael Morphew: born 1806 East Grinstead, parents Cripps Morphew flax draper & Mildred Morphew cook.
Matlida Morphew: born 1807 Rotherfield, parents William Morphew farmer & Mildred Morphew cook.
James Morphy: born 1807 Maresfield a broom maker, parents Thomas Morphy & Margaret Morphy.
Elizabeth Morphew: born 1807 Hartfield.
George Morphew: born 1808 East Grinstead, parent Cripps Morphew flax draper & Ann Morphew.
Harriet Morphew: born 1809 East Grinstead, parents Cripps Morphew flax draper & Ann Morphew
Thomas Morphey: born 1811 Maresfield a broom maker, Parents Thomas Morphy & Margaret Morphy.
Caroline Morphew: born 1812 East Grinstead, parents Cripps Morphew a Flax Draper & Ann Morphew.
Robert Morphew: born 1813 East Grinstead, parents Cripps Morphew a flax draper &Ann Morphew.
Elizabeth Morphew: born 1813 Middleton, parents Christopher Morphew a weaver and Elizabeth Morphw.

James Morphey: born 1814 Warbleton, parents Elizabeth Morphey a pauper.
Jane Morphew, 1816 baptised, East Grinstead, parents Cripps Morphew a flax draper & Ann Morphew.
Mary A. Morphey: born 1819 Warbleton.
Ephrain Morphey: born 1819 Warbleton.
Judith Hook Morphew: born 1820 Dicker, parents Thomas Morphy & Margaret Morphy.
William Morphew: born 1824 Dicker, parents Thomas Morphy & Margaret Morphy.
Jane Morphy: born 1826 Buxted.
Ann Morphew, 1828 baptised, Horsted Keynes, parents John Morphew servant /coachman & Mary Ann Morphew.
William Morphy: born 1830 Maresfield.
Mary Morphew: born 1830 Hartfield, parents George Morphew a shopkeeper and farmer & Elizabeth Morphew.
Frederick Morphew, 1830 baptised, Horsted Keynes.
John Morphew: born 1831 Isfield.
Elizabeth Morphew: born 1832 Hartfield, parents George Morphew a shopkeeper and farmer & Elizabeth Morphew.
John Morphew: born 1832 Hursted Keynes, parents John Morphew a servant and coachman & Mary Ann Morphew.
Fanny Morphy: born 1832 Maresfield, parents James Morphey a broom maker & Ann Morfey.
George Morphew: born 1833 Hartfield, parents George Morphew shopkeeper and farmer & Elizabeth Morphew.
Eliza Morphew: born 1833 Uckfield, parents John Morphew a servant and coachman & Mary Ann Morphew.
William Daniel Morphew, 1833 baptised, East Grinstead.

James Morfey: born 1834 Maresfield, parent James Morphy broom maker & Ann Morfey.

Margaret Morphew: born 1834 Frant, parents William Thomas Morphew & Susan Morphew.

Elizabeth Morphew: born 1836 East Grinstead.

Thomas Morphew: born 1837 Hartfield, parents George Morphew a shopkeeper and farmer & Elizabeth Morphew.

George Morfey: born 1837 Maresfield a stoker, parents James Morphy a broom maker & Ann Morfey.

Frederick Morphew: born 1837 Withyham, parents William Thomas Morphew & Susan Morphew.

William Morphy: born 1838 Maresfield, parents Thomas Morphey a broom maker & Sarah Ann Morphy.

George Morphew, 1838 baptised, Lewes.

Matilda Morphew: born 1839 Hartfield, parents George Morphew a shop keeper and farmer & Elizabeth Morphew.

Owen Morphy: born 1842 Maresfield, parents James Morphy broom maker & Ann Morfey.

Harriet Morphew: born 1844 Hartfield, parents George Morphew a shopkeeper and farmer & Elizabeth Morphew.

Harriet Morfey: born 1846 Maresfield, parents James Morphey broom maker & Ann Morfey.

Eileen Morphew: born 1846 Hartfield, parents George Morphew shopkeeper and farmer & Elizbeth Morphew.

Charles Morfey: born 1849 Maresfield, parents James Morphy broom maker & Ann Morfey.

Harry Morphey: born 1855 Nutley, parents James Morphy a broom maker & Ann Morfey.

Frances Morphew: born 1861 Rothersfield.

John Morphew, 1863 baptised, Lewes.

Martha Morphew, 1865 baptised, Lewes.
Grace Morphew, 1866 baptised, Lewes.
Rosina Morfew: born 1867, parents George Morfey a stoker & Mary Ann Morfew.

William Frederick Morphew: born 1867 Nutley, parents William Morphy & Elizabeth Morphew.
Ann Morphew: born 1867 Maresfield, parents William Morphy & Elizabeth Morphew.
Obed Alfred Morphew: born 1868 Buxted, parents Owen Morphy & Catherine Booker Morphew.
Harriet Annie Morphew: born 1869 Hartfield, parents John Morphew & Harriet Morphew.
Ralph Morphew, 1869 baptised, Lewes.
George Morphew: born 1870 Nutley, parents Owen Morphy & Catherine Brooker Morphew.
Emma Jane Morphew: born 1871 Maresfiled, parents William Morphy and Elizabeth Morphew.
George Morphew: born 1871 Hartfield, parents John Morphew & Harriet Ann Morphew.
Double Morphew, 1872 baptised, Fletching.
Louisa Morphew: born 1872 Nutley, Parents William Morphy & Elizabeth Morphew.
Fanny Morphew: born 1872 Hartfield, parents John Morphew & Harriet Ann Morphew.
Sarah Kate Morphew: born 1874 Maresfield, parents William Morphy & Elizabeth Morphew.
Henry John Morphew: born 1874 Hartfield, parents John Morphew & Harriet Morphew.
Marianne Morphew: born 1875 Buxted, parents Owen Morphy & Catherine Booker Morphew.
Albert Edward Morphew: born 1875 Nutley, parents William Morphy & Elizabeth Morphew.
Thomas Morphew: born 1875 Hartfield, parents Jhn Morphew & Harriet Ann Morphew.

Annie Morphew: born 1877 Maresfield, parents William Morphy & Elizabeth Morphew.
Elizabeth Morphew: born 1877 Hartfield, parents John Morphew & Harriet Ann Morphew.

Harriet Elizabeth Morphew: born 1878 Maresfield, parents William Morphy & Elizabeth Morphew.
Benjamin Morphew, 1878 baptised, Hastings.
Mary Eliza Morphew, 1879 baptised, Hastings.
Henry Morphew: born 1879 Buxted, parents Owen Morphy & Catherine Brooker Morphew.
Emily Morphew: born 1880 Hartfield, parents John Morphew & Harriet Ann Morphew.
Annie Jane Morphew, 1880 baptised, Hastings.
Edward Thomas Morphew: born 1881 Maresfield.
Fanny Morphew: born 882 Maresfield, parents William Morphy & Elizabeth Morphew.
Alfred Morphew: born 1882 Martfield, parents John Morphew & Harriet Ann Morphew.
Earnest George Morphew: born 1883 Maresfield, parents William Morphew broom maker & Elizabeth Morphew.
Esther Morphew: born 1883 Maresfield, parents Owen Morphy & Catherine Brooker Morphew.
Ellen Morphew: born 1884 Hartfield, parents John Morphew & Harriet Ann Morphew.
Albert Morphew: born 1886 Hartfield, parents John Morphew and Harriet Morphew.
Ernest Morphew: born 1886 Maresfield, parents John Morphy & Catherine Brooker Morphew.
Minnie Morphew: born 1887 Maresfiled, parents William Morphew.
Kate Morphew: born 1888 Hartfield, parents John Morphew & Harriet Ann Morphew.

Madelaine Morphew: born 1888 Maresfield, parents William Morphy & Elizabeth Morphew.
Winnifred Morphew: born 1891 Maresfiled, parents William Morphy & Elizbath Morphew.
Albert Morphew: born 1891 Maresfield, parents Owen Morphy & Catherine Brooker Morphew.

George William Morfield: born 1887, parents George William Morphew & Sarah Jane Morfield.
Allice Gertrude Morphew: born 1897 Buxted, parents Thomas William Frederick Morphew broom maker & Rebecca Morphew.
Charles Edward Morfield: born 1899.
Edith Mabel Morphew: born 1899 Buxted, parents Thomas William Frederick Morphew a broom maker & Rebecca Morphew.

Kent Morphews

Geoffrey Morphew, 1812 baptised, Gillingham.
James Shadrae? Morphew, 1815 baptised, Gillingham.
Jeremiah Morphew, 1818 baptised, Gillingham.
Sarah Anne Morphew, 1822 baptised, Gillingham.
William Morphew, 1822 baptised, Gillingham.
Marion Morphew: born 1838 Sevenoaks.
Augusta Morphew: born 1838 Malling.
Susanna Morphew: born 1840 Malling.
Charles Alfred Morphew: born 1840 Sevenoaks.
Frances Morphew: born 1840 Dover.
Sarah Jemima Morphew: born 1841 Medway
Amelia Maria Morphew: born 1842 Dover.
Charles Morphew: born 1843 Dover.
George Morphew: born 1845 Dover.
Elizabeth Ann Morphew: born 1845 Greenwich.
William Henry Morphew: born 1845 Dover/River.
William Morphew: born 1847 Malling.

Emma Morphew: born 1848 Greenwich.
William Henry Morphew: born 1848 Dover
Ann Morphew: born 1849 Malling.
Eliza Sophia Morphew: born 1849 Dover.
George Robert Morphew: born 1849 Malling.
Katherine Edith Morphew, 1849 baptised, Kemsing.
Selina H Morphew: born 1850 Malling.
Emma Carter Morphew: born 1850 Dover
Agnes Mary Morphew: born 1851 Lewisham.
Edward Morphew: born 1851 Malling.
Frederick Morphew: born 1852 Elham.
Philip Morphew: born 1852 Malling.
Edward Morphew: born 1853 Elham.
William Morphew: born 1853 Elham.
Augusta Lucy Morphew: born 1853 Lewisham.
Benjamin Love Morphew: born 1853 Dover.
Edmund Walter Morphew: born 1853 Malling.
Ellen Morphew: born 1854 Malling.
Alfred Nephi Morphew: born 1854 Dover.
George Edward Morphew: born 1854 Lewisham.
Frederick William Morphew: born 1855 Lewisham.
Annie Rosaline Millie Morphew: born 1855 Sevenoaks.
Amy Rosalind Morphew: born 1855 Malling, baptised Ightham.
George Thomas Morphew: born 1855 Elham.
Clara Morphew: born 1856 Greenwich.
Louisa Morphew: born 1856 Ashurst.
Louisa Morphew: born 1856 Malling.
Eliza Morphew: born 1857 Greenwich.
Rose Morphew: born 1857 Lewisham.
Emily Morphew; born 1857 Dover.
Agnes Amelia Morphew: born 1858 Dover.
Mary Morphew: born 1859 Sevenoaks.
Daniel Morphew: born 1859 Greenwich.
Emily Maud Minna Morphew: born 1859 Lewisham

Alice Gertrude Morphew: born 1859 Dover.
Alfred Baldock Morphew: born 1860 Dover.
Edwin Morphew: born 1860 Dover.
Edward Browning Morphew: born 1861 Dover.
Elizabeth Ann Morphew: born 1861 Greenwich.
Charles Morphew: born 1861 Elham.
Alfred Hatton Morphew: born 1861 Dover.
Harriet Ann Morphew: born 1861, place unknown.
James Edward Morphew: born 1861 Malling.
James Ellisson Morphew: born 1862 Malling.
Harriet Morphew: born 1862 Dover.
Alice Morphew: born 1863 Brasted.
Amy Catherline Morphew: born 1863 Malling.
Fanny Rosaline Morphew: born 1863 Malling.
Arthur Dennis Morphew: born 1863 Greenwich.
Alice Jane Morphew: born 1864 Malling, baptised Ightham.
William Henry Morphew: born 1864 Dover.
Frances Morphew: born 1865 Lewisham.
William Henry Morphew, 1865 baptised, Dover.
Margaret Elizabeth Morphew: born 1865 Elham.
George Edward Morphew: born 1865 Aylssham.
Emma Morphew: born 1865 Greenwich.
Henry Leslie Morphew: born 1866 Sevenoaks/Seal.
William Morphew: born 1866 Elham.
Annie Eliza Morphew: born 1866 Sevenoaks.
George E Morphew: born 1866 Malling.
Mary Ann Georgina Morphew, 1867 baptised, Strood.
Frederick Charles Morphew: born 1868 West Ashford.
Ellen Norah Morphew: born 1869 Dartford.
John Morphew: born 1869 Elham.
Augusta Ann Morphew: born 1870 Dartford.
George Frederick Morphew: born 1873, Canterbury.
Ellen Mera Morphew, 1873 baptised, Eynsford
Augustine Ann Morphew, 1873 baptised, Eynsford

Ellen Morphew: born 1876 Malling.
Edwin Oakenfull Morphew: born 1877 Bromley.
Emily Eliza Morphew: born 1877 Elham.
Philip George Morphew: born 1877 Dartford.
Emma Clara Morphew: born 1879 Bromley.
Florence Winifred Morphew: born 1879 Malling, baptisedd Ightham.
Edgar Gordon Morphew: born 1879 Elham.
Florence Morphew: born 1879 Dartford.
Lizzy Florence Morphew: born 1880 West Ashford.
Mabel Florence Morphew: born 1880 Elham.
Amy Stuart Morphew: born 1880 Tunbridge Wells.
Frederick Walter Morphew: born 1881 Malling.
Florence Amelia Morphew: born 1881 Greenwich.
Ellen Emily Morphew: born 1882 Elham.
Emily Anna Morphew: born 1882 Dartford.
Henry Morphew: born 1882 Malling.
William Thomas Morphew: born 1882 West Ashford.
Frances Morphew: born 1883 Malling.
William John Morphew: born 1883 Malling.
Rosa Mary Morphew: born 1884 Elham.
Thomas Ralph Morphew: born 1884 Malling.
Edmund Frank Morphew: born 1886 Malling.
Lilian Morphew: born 1887 Bromley.
Theresa Augusta Morphew: born 1887 Malling.
Ethel Kate Morphew: born 1887 Elham.
Holly Jane Morphew: born 1887 Gravesend.
Thomas Michael Morphew, 1888 baptised, Woolwich.
James Morphew: born 1888 Malling.
Violet Morphew: born 1888 Elham.
Lily Morphew: born 1888 Elham.
William Leslie Morphew: born 1889 Bromley.
John Morphew, 1889 baptised, Woolwich.
George Adame Morphew: born 1890 Woolwich.
Thomas CharlesMorphew: born 1890 Sevenoaks.
Madeline Morphew: born 1890 Elham.

Frederick Thomas Morphew: born 1891 Bromley.
Ralph Harold Morphew: born 1892 Woolwich.
Arthur Stanley Morphew: born 1894 Bromley.
Ethel Sophia M Morphew: born 1894 Malling.
Jesse George Morphew: born 1895 Bromley.
Fanny Winifred Morphew: born 1896 Woolwich.
Robert James, Morphew, 1896 baptised, Deptford.
Dorothy Queenie R Morphew: born 1897Bromley.
Gladys Alma Morphew: born 1897 Woolwich.
Edwin Leonard Morphew: born 1897 Bromley.
Florence Emily J. Morphew: born 1897 Elham.
Marie Rose Morphew: born 1897 Woolwich.
Dorothy Queenie Rose Morphew, 1897 baptised, Bromley Common.
Albert William Rex Morphew: born 1898 Bromley Common. Baptised Bromley Common.
Leslie Stanhope Morphew: 1898 baptised Woolwich.
Grace Emily Morphew: born 1898 Bromley.
Hilda Annie Morphew: born 1899 Bromley.
Hildred Olga Morphew: born 1899 Woolwich.
Daisy May C. Morphew: born 1899 Elham.
William Edwin Morphew: born 1899 Bromley.

Essex Morphews
John Morphew, 1804 baptised, Brentwood.
Elizabeth Morphew, 1805 baptised, Brentwood.
Henry Morphew, 1809 baptised, Romford.
Mary Morphew, 1810 baptised, Chelmsford.
Jane Morphew, 1813 baptised, Chelmsford.
John Morphew, 1834 baptised, Romford.
Marianne Sophia Morphew, 1836 baptised, Romford.

Suffolk Morphews

Joseph Morphew : born 1800, parents John and Sarah Morphew. married Mary Snell at Bildeston in 1828. Children; Susannah, Joseph, Mary, John, John, Betsey, William, Charles, Frederick, Robert.

John Morphew : born 1802 at Nedging. Parents John and Sarah Morphew.

James Morphew : born about 1805 at Nedging. Husbandman at Offton then Little Bicett. Married Esther 1834. Children, Esther, James, Georgena, Caroline, Frederick, Robert, John, Susanna, Maria, Mary Ann.

Elzabeth Morphew : born 1806 at Nedging.

John Marchant Morphew : born 1827 at Bildeston. A thatcher. Married Elizbeth Squirrel at Nedging. Children Elizabeth Mary, Susanna, John Walter, Robert William, Joshua, Peter.
Military record: service number 23485, 1914, 1916 and 1917 a Private serving in Suffolk Regiment.

Emma Morphew, 1830 baptised, Somersham.

George Morphew, 1830 baptised, Somersham.

William Morphew: born 1832 at Nedging, died Bildeston.

Mary Morphew: born 1835 at Nedging. Children; Josiah Morphew.

Sussanna Morphew : born 1837 at Nedging.
Elizabeth Mary Morphew born 1853. Married Charles Stow at Nedging

Josiah Morphew : born 1854 at Nedging. Parent Mary Morphew.

Thomas Morphew : born 1840 at Nedging.

Robert Morphew : born 1845 at Offton. Agricultural labourer. Married Jane Bradbrook in 1867. Children;

George, M.E., Caroline, Mary, Esther.
Susanna Morphew : born 1854 at Nedging.

Robert William Morphew : born 1856 at Nedging. Agricultural worker then a thatcher at Nedging. Married Ann Squirrel in 1877 at Nedging. Children Ada Elizabeth, Katie, Rose A., John R.
John Walter Morphew: born 1856 at Nedging. Farm labourer at Nedging then Watfield, Suffolk. Married Ellen Bramford in 1879. Children Earnest Walter, Herbert A., George F., Lilly M., Arthur William, Albert J., Edmund John. Married 2nd time to Kate Louise Burman 1913. Children Claude Walter.
Joshua Morphew : born 1858 at Nedging, Thatchers Boy at Nedging then agricultural labourer at Nedging. Married Susannah Lister in 1878 at Preston St. Mary, Suffolk. Children Frederick C., Rosanna.
Peter Morphew : born 1860 at Nedging. Agricultural labourer. Married Ellen Julia Knock in 1880 at Nedging
George Morphew : born about 1869 at Bildeston. Agricultural labourer at Nedging.
Caroline Morphew : born about 1875 at Bildeston. General servant (domestic) at Nedging.
Frederick Morphew : born 1879 at Nedging.
Ada Elizabeth Morphew : born 1879 at Nedging. Married Arthur William Death at Hitcham, Suffolk.
Oliver George Morphew : born about 1895 at Nedging. Died 1915 in Belgium.

Cambridgeshire Morphews (Huntingdonshire)
Mary Ann Morphew: born 1828, Cambridge.

Norfolk Morphews
Lydia Morphew, 1801 baptised, Costessey

John Cross Morphew, 1803 baptised, Walpole.
Mary Morphew, 1804 baptised, Costessey.

William Morphew, 1805 baptised, Great Ellingham.
Phoebe Morphew, 1807 baptised, Greta Ellingham.
George Valentine Morphew, 1807 baptised, Walpole.
Thomas Brigs Morphew, 1809 baptised, Great Ellingham.
Joseph Brigs Morphew, 1812 baptised, great Ellingham.
Thomas Morphew, 1820 baptised, Lakenham.
John Briggs Morphew, 1821, baptised, Great Yarmouth.
Caroline Morphew, 1821 baptised, Bridgham.
Susanna Morphew, 1821 baptised, Bridgham.
George Morphew, 1823 baptised, Bridgham.
Charlotte Morphew, 1827 baptised, Norwich.
Mary Ann Pheobe Morphew, 1831 baptised, Norwich.
Thomas Briggs Morphew, 1833 baptised, Norwich.
John Thomas Morphew, 1836 baptised, Great Yarmouth.
Samuel George Morphew, 1844 baptised, Great Yarmouth.
Henry James Morphew, 1854 baptised, Great Yarmouth.
William Charles Morphew, 1861 baptised, Great Yarmouth.
Ellen Matilda Morphew, 1869 baptised, Great Yarmouth.
Gertrude Clarissa Morphew, 1880 baptised, Great Yarmouth.

Clarissa Gertrude Morphew, 1881 baptised, Great Yarmouth.

Cornwall Morphews

Joseph Jeffery Morphew, 1809 baptised, Falmouth.
Francis Codd Morphew, 1811 baptised, Falmouth.
William Phillips Morphew, 1813 baptised, Falmouth.
Elizabeth Morphew, 1814 baptised, Falmouth.
Henry May Morphew, 1815 baptised, Falmouth.
Jeffery James Morphew, 1818 baptised, Falmouth.
Margaret Morphew, 1819 baptised, Falmouth.
Caroline Mary Morphew, 1820 baptised, Falmouth.

Lincolnshire Morphews

John Tomlinson Morphew, 1834 baptised, Horbling
Annette Sophia Morphew, 1838 baptised, Horbling.
James Morphew, 1843 baptised, Gainsborough.
Joseph Morphew, 1844 baptised, Gainsorough.
Susanna Morphew, 1846 baptised, Gainsborough.
Jane Ann Morphew, 1874 baptised, Cleethorpes.

Morphews of the 19th century who served in the British Army.

There are several records of Morphews who served in the British Army at www.british-army-records.co.uk. The earliest record in the 19th century is a John Morphew who served in the 18th Hussars at the Battle of Waterloo, 18th June 1815.

The official title for the regiment was 18th Kings Irish Regiment of Light Dragoons (Hussars).
Wellington served in this regiment as a young officer. The 18th Hussars served in The Peninsula, (Spain) under Wellington.

At Waterloo they were actively engaged during the battle. The 18th Hussars were on the left of Wellington's front line.
They were not commited to the battle until later in the day when they relieved the Scots Greys, (Royal Scots Dragoon Guards) and the 3rd Hussars, (Kings German Legion Regiment). These two regiments had been fighting through out the day. At one point the 18th Hussars charged French artillery protected by French Cuirassiers and Lancers. This charge was cheered by British Infantry squares and resulted in the capture of some French guns in limber, (hooked up). These guns were taken back to British lines.
The regiment then moved to the right of Wellington's front line where they encountered French artillery and cavalry when they charged several times. At one point the order to halt and reform was not heard and the light cavalry was accused of being 'ill disciplined'. Later French historians suggested that the British Light Cavalry charges helped bring about the defeat of Napoleon. At the start of the battle the 18th Hussars had 28 officers and 413 men. At the end the muster showed 13 men were killed, 2 officers and 72 men were wounded. 17 men were recorded as missing. After the battle the 18th Hussars were part of the British Army of Occupation Brigade with the 12th Lancers.
The 18th Hussars were disbanded in 1821.

Other records of Morphews serving in the British Army was James Morphew regimental number 3293 who

was as a private in 1851 in the 21st Royal Scots Fusiliers. Because of this date it can be assumed that James Morphew fought in the Crimean War, (1853-1856).
The 21st Royal Scots Fusiliers served through out the

war fighting at Alma where the British Army had to cross the Alma River and attack up the steep slopes to the Alma Heights. They were at Inkerman where British held off a huge Russian Army. The 21st were in the thick of the fighting holding the front line until French Zouaves arrived. During the siege of Sevastapol the Royal Scots were part of the first attacked the Redan, a fortified part of the Sevastapol defences. They were held in reserve on the second attack.
John Morphew regimental number 66273, regiment and rank unknown recorded in 1873.
A. E. Morphew, Regimental number D/22776 in 1884 was serving in the Royal Sussex Regiment. Possibly Arthur Ermes Morphew born in 1867 at Lambeth, London.
In 1890 there is a record of W. Morphew regimental number D40345 serving in the British Army.

American Morphew's

1801 Thomas Jefferson took office as President.

Aaron Morphew: born 1796 died 1860 in Arkansas, married Nancy Sample 1823. Parents Silas & Elizabeth Morphew.
James Morphew: born 1805 Elk Creek, Wilkes County, North Carolina. Married Rebecca Hogan in 1825 at Estill County, Kentucky. Parent Joseph Morphew.
1809 James Madison took office as President.
1811 Morphews left North Carolina. James Morphew Sr. and his son Joseph Morphew sold their land at Elk Creek to Ephriam Norris.

1817 James Munroe took office as President.

John Morphew: born 1823 died 1811, married Amanda Hawkins in Walker County Alabama. Later at Hot Springs, Clark County Arkansas.
1825 John Q. Adams took office as President.
Silas Morphew: born 1827 Walker County. Moved to Winston County Alabama, Wayne County Tennesee and Pike County Arkansas. Died 1906.
Elizabeth Morphew: born 1829 died 1895.
1829 Andrew Jackson took office as President
William H. Morphew: born 1829 at Putnam County, Indiana. Married Sarah Allumbaugh in 1846 at Fulton county, Illinois. Married Mary Anne Hines in 1876 at Woodburn, Iowa.

William H. Morphew and family moved frequently.
1829 – 1845 Putnam County Indiana
1845-1864 St. David, Fulton County, Illinois.
1850-? Wapello County Iowa
1864-1867 Greenbush, Warren County, Iowa.

1893 Haysville, Sedgwick County, Iowa.
1893 Woodburn, Clark County, Iowa.
1894-1897 Humeston, Wayne County, Iowa.
1897-1899 Conway, Laclede County, Missouri.
1899-1912 Garden City, Blue earth County, Minnesota.
William Morphew: born 1831.
Keziah Morphew: born 1833.
Solomon Morphew: born 1836 died 1908.
1837 Martin Van Buren took office as President.
1841 William H. Harrison took office as President.
1841 John Tyler took office as President.
Calvin Morphew: born 1842.
Nancy Jane Morphew: born 1843/44.
1845 James K. Polk took office as President.
Martha A. Morphew: born 1846/47.
Daniel Silas Morphew: born 1847 died 1929.
Gayner Prince Morphew: born 1848 died 1922.
Rebecca Morphew: born 1849.
1849 Zachary Taylor took office as President.
Mary Morphew: born 1850.
1850 Millard Fillmore took office as President.
William Thomas Morphew: born 1852 died 1931.
John F. Morphew: born 1852 died 1905.
Livinia K. Morphew: born 1852/53.
1853 Franklin Pierce took off as President.
Lunettie Jane Morphew: born 1854 died 1933.
Rebecca Ann Morphew: born 1854 died 1874.
Married John Ramsey.
Elizabeth Morphew: 1855/56.

William "Billie Pa" Albert Morphew: born 1856 died 1925.
Silas Buchanan Morphew: born 1856 died 1922.
John Riley Morphew: born 1857 died 1902.
William Elijah Morphew: born 1857, died ain infancy.
1857 James Buchanan took office as President.
Rosetta E. Morphew: born 1859 died 1926.
1861 Abraham Lincoln took office as President.
Parthenia Morphew: born 1862.
Rachel E. Morphew: born 1862 died 1864.
Harrison E. Morphew: born 1864 died 1870.
Martha M. Morphew: born 1864/65.
Eda Morphew: born 1865/66.
1865 Andrew Johnson took office as President.
Sarah A. Morphew: born 1866/67.
Martha E. Morphew: born 1866 died 1872.
Kerry A. Morphew: born 1867/68.
William Hiram Isiah Morphew: born 1867 died 1939.
1869 Ulysses S. Grant took office as President.
James Albert Morphew: born 1870 died 1947.
Seburn Asberry Morphew: born 1870 died 1930.
Charles Lee Morphew: born 1870 died 1942 at Lake Crystal, Minnesota. Married May Evan. They had three children.
Nancy N. Morphew: born 1872/73.
John Thomas Morphew: born 1874 died 1957.
Sophonia C. Morphew: born 1876/77.
1877 Rutherford B Hayes took office as President.
Marion H. Morphew: born 1877 at Woodburn, Iowa. Died 1964 Minneapolis, Minnesota. Married Celia Ann Lee. Had five children.
Joseph A. Morphew: born 1877/78.
Rachel J. Morphew: born 1878 died 1920. Married Robert Harvey.
David Montgomery Morphew: born 1879 died 1966.

Lucy E. Morphew: born 1880 died 1976. Married Arthur William Eaton.
1881 James A. Garfield took office as President.
Veturia M. Morphew (Dolly): born 1881 died 1962.
1881 Chester A. Arthur took office as President.
1885 Grover Cleveland took office as President.

Geralda May Morphew: born 1888. Parents Charles Lee and May Morphew.
Lilly Ocean Morphew: born 1889. Parents Charles Lee and May Morphew.
1889 Benjamin Harrison took Office as President.
1893 Grover Cleveland took office as President.
Orre M. Morphew: born, date unkown. Parents Charles Lee and May Morphew.
1897 William McKinley took office as President.

Morphews who served in the American Army

A James Morphew was listed as serving during the 1812 War against the British Colony of Canada. He is recorded as being from Ohio.
At the out break of the American Civil War in 1861 the armies in the North and South were relatively small. The First Battle of Bull Run, (First Battle of Manassas) was a modest battle compared to those that took place in Europe and later battles of the Civil War. But after the battle many joined the armies of both sides including Morphews. They were from a number of states both north and south. Some names appear to be the same person. This could be where a regiment had been so depleted that a new one was formed and the individual joined the new regiment, in particular is Enos A. Morphew was born c 1838 at Shelby County Indiana volunteered for the Union Army in 1862 at Peoria Illanois. There is a record of Enos volunteering two more times. He died in 1922.

Josiah B. Morphew was born c 1824 at Knox County, Tennessee. He enlisted in 1862 and was a resident on Saline County Illinois. Recorded on a soldier and prisoner list.
Garner P. Morphew was a resident of Arkansas. He died 1922.

Seaborn H. Morphew of Arkansas, he enlisted in the Confederate Army.
Levi Morphew of North Carolina.
J. Morphew of Arkansas,
Elichu or Elihu A. Morphew of Arkansas. Also found on a soldier and prisoner record.
Jesse Y. Morphew of Tennesee. Also found on a soldier and prisoner record.
Josiah Morphew of Illonois, also recorded of Kentucky.
John Morphew of Indiana. Found on a soldier and prisoner record list.
John C. Morphew of Missouri. Enlisted 1863 at Fayette Indiana
Germiah Morphew of Arkansas,.
James B Morphew of Missouri.
S.G. Morphew of Tennesee.
Solomon Morphew of Arkansas, joined the Confederate Army.
John Morphew of Arkansas.
Silas Morphew, a southern loyalist..
John G. Morphew of Kenucky.
Gerymial Morphew
J. W. Morphew.
Jesee H. Morphew.
Paran Morphew of Alabama. Confederate pension and service.
Simean Morphew enlisted 1863 at Fayette, Indiana.
David Morphew enlisted 1863 at Hendricks, Indiana.
Ransom Morphew. Enlisted 1863 at Bremer, Iowa.

J. W. Morphew.
S. Morphew of Waxtanga, North Carolina. Pardoned under the Proclomation of 1865-1869. This pardon was issued by the President for all those who rebelled excepted under the charge of treason or other felonies.
James MacDonald Morphew, 1867-1946

Thomas Arthur Morphew 1867-1944
On April 25th war broke out between America and Spain. Three Morphews served in this war . Private Frank C. Morphew of Illinois and Private Frank E. Morphew also of Illinois. Maybe they are one of the same person. Also Private Eden L. Morphew of Iowa.

Canadian Morphews

D.W. Morphew: born about 1828, 1851 census living in Hamilton, Ontario.

Hannah Morphew: born about 1832, 1851 census Hamilton, Ontario.

Jane Morphew: born about 1850, 1851 census Hamilton, Ontario.

Gusta Morphew: born 1886, 1911 census Renfrew, Ontario.

Morphews who served in Canadian armed forces pre 1900.
E Morphew, Volunteer Militia
Joseph Morphew, served 1803 to 1815.

Morffew

At the end of the 18th Century the name Morffew appears in Kingston, (Kingston upon Thames) records. There is no obvious reason why the name should change from Morphew to Morfew and then Morffew except for an aversion to baptising an individual with a name of the skin affliction 'morphew'. It could also be a genuine spelling mistake that started a new name.
The Morffew families recorded in Kingston on Thames, Surrey migrated to London, especially in the Chelsea area but there are records across London, primarily in Surrey London and Berkshire.
Kingston upon Thames formed an ancient parish in the Kingston hundred of Surrey.

The Parish of Kingston upon Thames covered a large area including Hook, Kew, New Malden, Petersham, Richmond and Surbiton. Many large manors were built here in the Tudor period such as Hampton Court. Kingston on Thames was one of the few places that had a bridge crossing the River Thames, a strategic point during the English Civil War.
In 1801 Thomas Morffew joined the Ancient Society of College Youths. This was a bell ringing society that was established in 1637. Thomas lived in Kingston upon Thames.
In the 19th century Morffews moved to Chelsea. In the late 17th century Chelsea was a popular location for the wealthy and described as "a village of palaces" with a population of 3,000. Chelsea remained rural and served London as a market garden, a trade that continued until the 19th-century when there was a development boom The district eventually was absorbed into the metropolis.

In the reign of James I Mulberry Trees were planted in various places around London including Chelsea. This was in hope to start a silk industry. Silk worms feed on Mulberry leaves but only of the white variety. Inadvertantley Black Mulberries were planted instead and the silk worm project failed.
King's Road was named for Charles II, recalling the King's private road from St James's Palace to Fulham, which was maintained until the reign of George IV.
In the mid 19th century Several morffews emigrated to Australia.

Surrey Morffews
Mary Morffew: born 1801 place unknown, parents Thomas and Hannah Morphew.

Sarah Morffew: born 1804 place unknown, parents Thomas and Hannah Morphew.
John Morffew: born 1818, parents Richard and Harriet Morffew.
Henry George Morffew: born 1819 Kingston on Thames, parents Henry and Sarah Morffew.
Henry Morffew: born 1820 Ham, Kingston on Thames, parents Henry and Sarah Morffew, Married Ann Griffiths Kennington 1847, died 1874 Chelsea.
Mary Ann Morffew: born 1822 Kingston on Thames, parents Henry and Sarah Morffew.
George Morffew: born 1822 Kingston on Thames, parents William James and Elizabeth Morffew.
Elizabeth Morffew: born 1824 Kingston on Thames, parent Henry and Sarah Morffew.
Harriet Morffew: born 1827 Kingston on Thames, parents Henry and Sarah Morffew.
HannahMorffew: born 1828 Kingston on Thames, parents William James and Elizabeth Morffew.

James Morffew: born 1828 Kingston on Thames, parents William James and Elizabeth Morffew.
Charlotte Morffew: born 1829 Kingston on Thames, parents Henry and Sarah Morffew.
Robert Samuel Morffew: born 1877 Kingston on Thames.
Frederick George Morffew: born 1878 Kingston on Thames. Military service; service number 249235 1914 Labour Corps, 1917 301st Labour Corps.
Robert Samuel Morffew: born 1880 Kingston on Thames.
Alice Jane Morffew: born 1882 Kingston on Thames.
Henry Morffew: born 1883 Kingston on Thames.
Henry Morffew: born 1884 Richmond.
William Morffew: born 1885 Kingston on Thames.

Elizabeth Morffew: born 1886 Kingston on Thames, died 1887.
George Morffew: born 1887 Kingston. 1911 census at Chelsea.
William Morffew: born 1887 Kingston on Thames.
Charlotte Morffew; born 1889 Kingston on Thames.
Rose Morffew: born 1891 Richmond.
William Walter Morffew: born 1896 Richmond.

Berkshire Morffews
Elizabeth Morffew: born 1850 Reading.
George Morffew: born 1856 Reading.
Arthur John Morffew: born 1860, Reading.
Louise Mary Morffew: born 1862, Reading.
Fanny Eliza Morffew: born 1865, Reading.
Walter William Morffew: born 1884 Reading. Military service; service number 31492, 1916 recorded as being in the Royal Air Force. In 1918 was a private.
Katherine Louise Morffew: born 1886, Reading.

London Morffews
William John Morffew: born 1819 London, married Mary Ann Horwood in 1848 at Shadwell. William was a Lastmaker.
Thomas Morffew: born 1822 place unknown married Sarah Aitkenhead in 1841 Westminster.
George Morffew: born 1822 Hackney.
Sarah Morffew: born 1830 Westminster, emigrated to Australia in 1852
Elizabeth Morffew: born 1832 Westminster, died 1836 Westminster.
Maria Morffew: born 1835 Westminster, Emigrated to Australia in 1852
Henrietta Morffew: born 1839 Westminster.

Emily Ann Morffew: born 1842 Westminster
Harriet Ann Morffew: born 1842 Westminster.
Thomas Morffew: born 1845 St Martins in the Fields.
Emma Ann Morffew: born 1846 St Martins in the Fields.
Henry Morffew: born 1847 Chelsea, parents Henry and Ann Morffew, died 1918 Chelsea.
Mary Anne Morffew: born 1848 Hanover Sq.
Ann Maria Morffew: born 1849 Chelsea.
Anna Maria Morffew: born 1850 St Martins in the Fields.
Elizabeth Morffew: born 1850 Chelsea, died 1860.
Elizabeth Jane Morffew: born 1850 Shadwell.
Alfred James Morffew: born 1852 Shadwell
Robert Morffew: born 1852 Chelsea, parents Henry and Anne Morffew, died 1854 Chelsea.
Robert Walter Morffew: born 1854. a Postman. Convicted at the Old Bailey for stealing a postal order of 15 shillings. Sentenced to one year hard labour, other record mentions being transported.

Henry William Morffew: born 1854 Holborn
Alice Morffew: born 1854 Chelsea, parents Henry & Ann Morffew.
Mary Ann Morffew: born 1855 Westminster, parents Henry and Ann Morffew.
Emily Morffew: born 1856 Clerkenwell.
George Morffew: born 1856 Paddington.
George Walter Morffew: born 1856 Shadwell
Mary Ann Morffew: born 1856 Chelsea
Mary Morffew: born 1858 Islington
Emma Alice Morffew: born 1858 Shadwell
James Morffew: born 1859 Islington

Emily Morffew: born 1859 Chelsea, parents Henry and Ann Morffew.
George Morffew: born 1862 Islington, died 1863.
Sarah Morffew: born 1862 Chelsea, parents Henry and Ann Morffew: married John William Dring 1882 Chelsea.
Harriet Morffew: born 1864 Chelsea, parents Henry and Ann Morffew: died 1865 Chelsea.
Edmund Morffew: born 1866 West London
Edmund Joshua Morffew: born 1867 Hackney. Died 1871.
Eliza Morffew: born 1867 Chelsea, parents Henry and Ann Morffew.
Lilly Ann Morffew: born 1871 Chelsea, parents Henry and Ann Morffew.
Thomas Purvis Morffew: born 1872 Hanover Sq.
Mary Ann Morffew: born 1874 Chelsea, parents Henry and Annie Morffew, died 1874.
Lydia Louisa Morffew: born 1875 Chelsea, parents Henry and Annie Morffew: died 1876 Chelsea.
Emily Errington Morffew: born 1876 Hanover Sq

Henry James Morffew: born 1876 Chelsea, parent Henry and Annie Morffew.
Military service; service number 98698, 1914 was a driver in Royal Field Artillery. 1917 a driver in Royal Field Artillery. A driver was equivalent to the rank of private. He drove the team of horses that pulled the artillery guns. Died 1940
Thomas Crowther Morffew: born 1877 Chelsea, parents Henry and Annie Morffew.
Emma Lizzie Morffew: born 1878 Kensington
Robert Morffew: born 1879 Chelsea, parents Henry and Annie Morffew, died 1879.
Maud Eliza Morffew: born 1879 St. Pancras

Alfred Morffew: born 1880 Chelsea, parents Henry and Annie Morffew, died 1880.
Thomas Morffew: born 1881 Chelsea, parents Henry and Annie Morffew died 1881.
Emily Elizabeth Morffew: born 1882 Chelsea, parents Henry and Annie Morffew.
Ethel Eliza Morffew: born 1883 St. Pancras, died 1886 Pancras.
Emma Mary Morffew: 1884 Chelsea, parents Henry and Annie Morffew.
Marthe Frances Morffew: born 1886 St Pancras
George Morffew: born 1886 Chelsea, parents Henry and Annie Morffew.
Gertrude Lilian Morffew: born 1887 St. Pancras
James William Morffew: born 1888 Islington.
William Morffew: born 1888 Chelsea, parents Henry and Annie Morffew, died 1888.
Eliza Rose Morffew: born 1890 Chelsea, parents Henry and Annie Morffew.

George Henry Morffew: born 1890 St. Pancras. Military service; two records for a George H. Morffew. Both served in the London Regiment in 1914, both privates. One service number is 2132 and another 205896.
Edward Morffew: born 1892 Chelsea, parents Henry and Annie Morffew.
Elizabeth Ellen S. Morffew: born 1893 Wandsworth.
Frances Lilian Morffew: born 1894 St. Pancras
Arthur John Morffew: born 1895 Chelsea, parents Henry and Annie Morffew, died 1967 Kensington. Military service; One record has a Arthur J. Morffew service number 1718 as a private in the London Regiment. Three other records show as service

number 408417 in the Royal air Force. 1914 as a private. In 1918 as a air mechanic 2nd class and again in 1918 as a air mechanic 3rd class.

Eve Magdalaine Morffew: born 1896 St. Pancras, died 1897 St. Pancras.

William Keates Morffew: born 1899 Islington. Military service; service number 37808, 1914 recorded as being a private in the Suffolk Regiment. 1918 was a private in Cambridgeshire Regiment.

Gloucestershire Morffews

Earnest Charles Morffew: born 1889 Stroud, died 1889.

Australian Morffews

Thomas Morffew was born in 1794 at Kingston on Thames, Surrey, Britain.

He married Sarah Collins at St. Martins in the Fields on 26th December 1814. St. Martins in the Fields is in London, a prominent well known church that is today by Trafalgar Square.

He later married Elizabeth Lee who was born in 1798 in Soho, West London in 1821. Soho at the time was a respectable area of London where affluent middle class people lived.

Thomas Morffew, with his two wives had five children. Maria Morffew born 1836 London, she married John

Pattie; Elizabeth Morffew born 1828 at St. James, Westminster, London; Rosina Morffew born in 1826 at St James, Westminster, London and died in 1846; Mary Ann Morffew born 1823 Newington, Surrey and Thomas Morffew born 1822 at Soho, he married Sarah Ann who died in 1862.

In 1852 Sarah and Maria Morffew immigrated to Australia on the Apoline

Thomas and Sarah had six children. Thomas Morffew who was baptised at St. Martins in the Fields on June 25th 1845; William Morffew born 1845 and baptised at St Martin in the Fields and Thomas Morffew born 1847 and baptised at St Anne, Soho, London.

In the mid 1850 the rich who had lived and frequented the area of Soho moved out. Music halls and theatres opened, Soho and the surrounding area became seedier attracting prostitutes. Thomas and Sarah Morffew with their three children decided to immigrate to Australia and settled in Victoria.

Here they had three of their six children. Henry Filgate Morffew born in 1854 at Collingwood, Victoria. Collingwood is now a suburb of Melbourne; Sarah Ann

Morffew born in 1855 at Chilwell, Victoria. Chilwell is on Port Phillip Bay, the same bay as Melbourne.

Annie Maria Morffew, born in 1856 at Ballarat, Victoria. It was at this time that there was a goldrush at Ballarat which started in 1851 and lasted until the late 1860s. Ballarat became a wealthy town having the highest gold out put of any where else at the time. The highest yield was in 1856, just about the time when several Morphews were born in Ballarat. The gold prospected at Ballarat was exported along with the other gold rush encampments in Victoria to Britain via Melbourne which benefited from this new wealth.

Thomas Morffew trained as a dental doctor in Melbourne. Later Thomas immigrated to San Francisco, California, America. It was the time of the gold rush but Thomas does not seem to be involved in any gold prospecting. Thomas and Margaret had a daughter called Alice.

One of Thomas's siblings, Henry Filgate Morffew married Annie Way. They appear to have had twelve children. Henry Thomas Morffew born in 1874 in Melbourne North and had a son called Charles; Arthur James Morffew born in 1875 at Hotham; Florence Emily Morffew born in 1875 at Hotham and had a daughter, Elizabeth; Alfred George Morffew born in 1879 and died the same year; Ernest Filgate Morffew born 1879 and died the same year; Maria Annie Morffew born 1880 and died the same year; John Ringland Morffew born 1881 and died the same year, Alice Victoria Morffew born 1883 at Hotham and died the same year; William Frederick Morffew born 1887; Annie Elizabeth Morffew born 1892 at Carlton and died 1892; Edith Morffew born 1890 at Carlton, Victoria and died the same year Albert Victor Morffew born 1895 and died in 1972; Leslie William Morffew born 1898, he

married Elvie Victoria Oakley and died 1967, they had three children Beryl P., Annie S. and Mary L.

A number of Henry and Annie Morffews children not only died at an early age but there does not appear to be a record of where they were born. This could be construed that Henry was an itinerant worker at some stage.

Other Morffews in Australia
Edmond James Morffew: born 1864 Ballarat Victoria. Died 1939 Ballarat.

Eliza Jane Morffew: born 1873 Victoria, died 1920.
Henrietta Elizabeth Morffew: born 1876 Ballarat Victoria, married 1895.
Henry Morffew: record 1878 of a petty session (court case for a minor crime) in Victoria.
Edward Frederick Morffew: born 1887 Victoria.
Edith Lillian Morffew: born 1891 Victoria.
Edith Caroline Morffew: born 1893 Victoria, died 1981.

American Morffews

As previously mentioned Thomas Morffew immigrated to San Francisco, California. Thomas Morffew is recorded in the 1880 US Federal census.
San Francisco was expanding at this time, Thomas Morffew resided at the Cosmopolitan Hotel which was destroyed in the 1906 San Francisco earth quake which also destroyed much of the city.
In 1881 Thomas Morffew Married Mary Peel, the widow of Johnathan Peel, the brother of Robert Peel the British Prime Minister. She had three sons and two

servants. She was of good means having inherited her father's estate valued at a million dollars and that of her deceased husband.

Thomas was popular with the children and one was to become a dental surgeon as well. These children adopted Thomas's family name, (Morffew) as their middle name.

Thomas Morffew

In 1874 he entered the medical department of the University of California, where he remained during the years 1874-5, at the same time keeping up his connection in the dental profession. In 1882 he entered the dental department of the same university, and graduated at that institution in the same year, receiving his Doctor of Dental Surgery.

Dr. Morffew was the first president of the Alumni of the dental department of the University of California, and also vice-president of the California State Odontological Society. He was twice appointed by the Governor of California as a member of the California Board of Dental Examiners; was elected by the members of that board as its president; was for six years secretary of the San Francisco Dental Association; was elected by the members of that association as its president and became a member of the California State Dental Association and one of its trustees. Thomas Morffew became president of the association.

20th Century & 21st

In 1900-1901 Reginald Morphew was commissioned by G.F. Harrington an auctioneer and surveyor to design a block of residential chambers at Jermyn Street, London. Jermyn Street is in Central London just off Piccadilly Circus.

Reginald Morphew submitted his designs to the Crown surveyors who found them 'quaint' and 'bald'. These new buildings had an 'Art Nouveau' influence.

The buildings had a shop and a woollen warehouse.

1901 Queen Victoria died at Osborne House on the Isle of Wight, she was succeeded by Edward VII.

Edward VII died in 1910 at Buckingham Palace, he was succeeded by George V.

Sussex deeds to land in 1912 refers to Henry Cosmo Orme Bosnor conveyed to Edward Standen Morphew, representative of Walton Heath Land Ltd the Warren Farm Estate……..Trustees of Morphew conveyed adjacent land owned by Edward Standen Morphew.

In 1925 Warren Farm at Kingswood, Surrey auctioned 185 acres through Edward Standen Morphew.

Kingswood is recorded in the Domesday Book and says that Kingswood was held by William I. Kingswood was held independent of the land around it but Henry VIII seized Kingswood Manor and the land. Henry annexed it to Hampton Court.

Elizabeth I bestowed Kingswood to Lord Howard of Effingham but was later sold by his grand son. William Cromwell bestowed Kingswood to a loyal roundhead cavalier.

Kingswood exchanged hands several times prior to the 19th century. Kingswood was bound in the east by Gatton.

Until the early 20th century Kingswood was part of the 'Kingswood Liberty'.
A Liberty was region in a county that was independent of surrounding hundreds and Boroughs and held as private land.
Kingswood comprised of 1,821 acres, 400 acres was woodland and the rest arable land.

Harold Morphew of Loxwood Place, Loxwood joined the Sussex Archialogical Society in 1913, possibly the Harold Morphew who was born 1880 Wandsworth, Surrey.
In 1914 Mr. Allan L Morphew bought Brightwell Manor, (Oxfordshire) from Reverend William Toovey whose family had owned it for 150 years. Allan Morphew seems to have resided at this manor for a short period and sold it on.
Frederick George Morffew, possibly the same Frederick George Morffew born in 1878 at Ham near Richmond and Kingston on Thames. He volunteered to join the British Army at the out break of WWI. He was turned down for being deaf. Later in the war he volunteered again and was accepted for the Labour Corps digging trenches and tunnels. Frederick was killed on 18th October 1917 at Ypes. His service record shows him as a Private 249235. He is buried in Talana Farm Cemetary Belgium B. 85.
Frederick did not have to volunteer but many who were in the same situation found they were shunned by society for supposedly being cowards. As many did across the British Empire he felt obliged to fight for King and Country.

Others who served during World War I were Private John Marchant Morphew who was born in Nedging, Suffolk, he served in the 7th Suffolk Regiment and was killed in action on 10th April 1917, regt no 23485. Private George Edward Morphew, he was born in Nedging in 1880. He served with the 34th Labour Corp then later transferred to 101st Company Regiment. He died of his wounds in 1918 at Rouen. Georges two brothers also fought in WWI They were Private Albert P. Morphew who served in the Artillery and Private Bert W. Morphew who was in the Expeditionary Force.

1936 George V died at Sandringham House, he was succeeded by Edward VIII. Edward abdicated that same year and George VI took the throne.

1952 George VI died at Sandringham House. He was succeeded by Queen Elizabeth II.

Maufes

Frederick Broadbent Muff was born in 1857. Edward Brantwood Muff who was born in 1882 at Sunny Bank, Ikley, Yorkshire.

The family moved to Chelsea London.

In 1909 the family name was changed to Maufe by deed pole.

Thomas Harold Broadbent Maufe was Edward's cousin, Thomas's siblings were Frederick William Broadbent Maufe, Stratham Broadbent Maufe.

Thomas Harold Broadbent Maufe served in World War I with 124th Seige Artillery and won the Victoria Cross. Thomas died in 1942.

Edward Brantwood Maufe joined the army in 1917 and served during World War I in the Royal Garrison

Artillery. He went on to become a celebrated architect. He died in 1974.

Other Maufes
Inger-Lise C. Maufe born in 1956, Norfolk.
Anthony Micheal Maufe, born 1946, Yorkshire.
Miranda Maufe born in 1942, Norfolk.
Ambrose Gordon Maufe, born 1927, Yorkshire.
Oliver Gordon Maufe born 1923, Yorkshire.
Garry Humphries Maufe, born 1922, York.
David Humphris Maufe, born 1919, Yorkshire.
Gabriel Gordon Maufe, born 1919, Yorkshire.
Simon Maufe, born 1917, Yorkshire
Michael Humphris Maufe, born 1916, Yorkshire.
Amanda Giselle Maufe, born 1953, Middlesex.
Maufes appear in American records.
Rachel Armstronge Maufe, born 1926, Cattarauges, New York.
Gareth Piers Danvers Maufe, born 1911, Suffolk County, Massachusetts.

Surrey Morphews

Raymond Morphew: born 1901 Croydon.
Raymond Morphew: born 1901 Norwood.
Leslies Morphew: born 1902 Kingston.
Lillian Morphew: born 1903 Dulwich.
Margaret Morphew: born 1905 Dulwich.
Henry George Schofield Morphew: born 1906 Streatham.
Elsie Mabel Morphew: born 1907 West Surrey.
Rhoda Morphew: born 1908 South Surrey.
Frances Emily Mary Morphew: born 1908 Streatham.
Emily Jane E. Morphew: born 1909 Farnham.
Marjorie Morphew: born 1909 East Surrey.
Ivy Gladys Morphew: born 1909 North West Surrey
Ruth Oliver Morphew: born 1909 Croydon.
John Ernest Morphew: born 1909 Kingston (Kingston upon Thames).
John Ernest Morphew: born 1910 New Malden.
Chrisopher S. Morphew: born 1911 Godstone.
Arthur James Morphew: born 1911 Croydon.
Florence D. Morphew: born 1917 Croydon.
Arthur Edward B Morphew: born 1919 North West Surrey.
Theodore G. Morphew: born 1923 Farnham.
Edward S. Morphew: born 1923 Guildford.
Stanley J. Morphew: born 1924 Croydon.
Walter Joseph Morphew: born 1926 West Surrey.
Mary Morphew: born 1930 Reigate.
David E. Morphew: born 1931 Croydon.

David J. Morphew: born 1931 Croydon.
John A. A. Morphew: born 1934 East Surrey.
Albert S. R. Morphew: born 1937 East Surrey.
Robert A. Morphew: born 1938 East Surrey.
Ann V. Morphew: born 1939 East Surrey.
Kenneth J. Morphew: born 1942 East Surrey.
David C. Morphew: born 1945 East Surrey.
Ann E. Morphew: born 1948 North East Surrey.
Robert H. Morphew: born 1949 East Surrey
Alan L. Morphew: born 1952 South East Surrey.
Andrew S. Morphew: born 1952 North east Surrey.
Denise P. Morphew: born 1954 East Surrey.
David J. Morphew: born 1954 North East Surrey.
Jacqueline A. Morphew: born 1955 East Surrey.
Rosemary E. Morphew: born 1955 East Surrey
Christopher Morphew: born 1960 South West Surrey.
John A. Morphew: born 1962 West Surrey.
Ian David Morphew: born 1966 South Surrey.
Elizabeth Mary Morphew: born 1966 Croydon.
Louise Jane Morphew: born 1967 Croydon.
Geoffrey Charles Morphew: born 1970 Merton.
Carl Robert A. Morphew: born 1973 South East Surrey.
Alison Susan Morphew: born 1973 Croydon.
Scott Patrick Morphew: born 1975 Croydon.
Lisa Marie Morphew: born 1978 Sutton.
Kim Elizabeth Morphew: born 1979 East Surrey.
Russell Mark Morphew: born 1979 Sutton.
Ben Robert Morphew: born 1981 Mid East Surrey.

Samuel Luke Morphew: born 1996 South East Surrey.
Connor Joseph Morphew: born 1998 West Surrey.

Sussex Morphews

Frederica Jane Morphew: born 1900, Buxted.
William James Morphew: born 1900, Buxted.
Thomas Ardon Ambrose Morphew: born 1900, Maresfield. Parents, Harding Ambrose Dadswell a Labourer & Emily Morphew.
Frederick Morfield: born 1901. Parents, George William Morphew & Sarah Jane Morphew.
Winifred Mary Morphew: born 1902 Buxted. Parents, Thomas William Frederick Morphew a broom maker & Rebecca Morphew.
Ethal Morffew: born 1904 Battersea. Died 1974 Colchester.
Florence Mary Morphew: born 1904 Chailey. Parents, Double Morphew & Clara Morphew.
Ena Patricia Morphew: born 1906 Buxted. Parents, Thomas William Frederick Morphew a broom maker & Rebecca Morphew.
Edith Bertha Morphew: born 1907 Brighton. Parents Henry Morphew & Rebecca Morphew.
George Ernest Morphew: born 1908 Buxted. Parents, Thomas William Frederick Morphew a broom maker & Rebecca Morphew.
Beatrice Nellie Morphew: born 1908 Hartfield, died 5th July 1997. Parents Alfred Morphew & Maria Morphew.

Catherine F. Morphew: born 1910 Brighton. Parents, Henry Morphew & Charlotte Bertha Morphew.
Florence Margaret Morfield: born 1910 Portslade. Parents, George William Morfield & Martha Marfield.
Ethel Morphew: born 1910.
Alfred John Morphew: born 1910 Hartfield. Parents Alfred Morphew & Maria Morphew.
Charles Horace Morphew: born 913 Hartfield: Parents Alfred Morphew and Maria Morphew.
Rhoda Morphew: born 1915 Hartfield.
Emily Morphew: born 1915 Hartfield. Parents, Alfred Morphew & Maria Morphew.
William Thomas Morphew: born 1918 Hartfield. Parents, Alfred Morphew & Maria Morphew.
Beatrice Margaret Mary Morphew: born 1920 Hartfield.
Elsie Morphew: born 1920 Hartfield.
Elsie Irene Morphew: born 1921 died 1986. Parents, Alfred Morphew & Maria Morphew.
Margaret Joan Morphew: born 1921 Hartfield. Parents, Alfred morphew & Maria Morphew.
Jean Mary Morphew: born 1921 Hartfield. Parents, Alfred Morphew & Maria Morphew.
John Morphew: born 1930 Hartfield. Parents, Alfred John Morphew & Ethel Morphew.
Robert Morphew: born 1930 Hartfield: Parents, Alfred John Morphew & Ethel Morphew.
Stephen Paul Reuben Morphew: born 1940 Hartfield. Parents, William Thomas Morphew & Beatrice Margaret Mary Morphew

Suffolk Morphews and Morphey

Stanley C Morphey: born 1900.
Sidney E Morphey: born 1900.
Arthur A. Morphew: born 1901.
Margaret Morphew: born 1902.
William C. Morphew: born 1902.
Cara E. Morphew: born 1902.
Henry C. Morphew: born 1902.
Phillip Morphey: born 1903
Ellen L. Morphew: born 1903
Claude C Morphey: born 1903
Nelson Morphew: born 1905.
Horatio J. W. Morphew: born 1905
Ella M Morphew: born 1905.
Ivy Morphey: born 1905.
Gladys Ena Morphey: born 1906.
Violet W. Morphew: born 1906.
Cyril H. Morphew: born 1907.
Hilda M. Morphew: born 1907.
Hilda J. Morphew: born 1907.
Doris A. Morphew: born 1907.
Alfred R Morphew: born 1907.
Herbert J. Morphew: born 1908.
Charles W. Morphew: born 1909
Charles H. Morphey: born 1909.
Grace E. Morphew: born 1909.
Dorothy Maud Morphey: born 1910.
Howard H. Morphy: born 1910
Violet E. Morphew: born 1910.
Edmund J. Morphew: born 1910.

Florence E. Morphew: born 1910.
Jessica M. Morphew: born 1910
George V. Morphew: born 1911
Frederick G. Morphew: born 1911.
Eva Gertrude Morphew: born 1912.
Ruby F. Morphew: born 1912.
Phylis Morphy: born 1913.
Ralph H Morphew: born 1913.
Edward T. Morphey: born 1914.
Stanley W. Morphew: born 1914.
Herbert E. Morphew: born 1914.
Donald G. Morphew: born 1914.
Winifred M. Morphew: born 1915.
Dorothy E. Morphew: born 1915.
Ernest A. Morphew: 1915.
Leonard C. Morphew: born 1916.
William H Morphew: born 1916
Frederick C. Morphew: born 1919
Edith M. Morphew: born 1922.
Raymond L. Morphey: born 1923.
Reginald C.E. Morphew: born 1926.
Edward Morphy: born 1926
Peter T. B. Morphew: born 1927.
Russell N. Morphew: born 1929.
Christopher Morphew: born 1930
Edward G Morphew: born 1930
Rita E. Morphew: born 1932.
Maisie Dorren Morphew: born 1932.
Edwin D. Morphey: born 1933
Bernard E. Morphew: born 1935.

Ronald C. Morphew: born 1937.
Rose Morphy: born 1937.

Cambridgeshire, (Huntingdonshire) Morphews
Florence Lilian Mary Morphew: born 1940 at Mepal.
Gladys Edith Morphew: born 1947 at Sutton.

Kent Morphews
Ivy Alice Morphew, 1900 baptised, Woolwich/Deptford

Morphew military service with United Kingdom armed forces, pre-1919

Like many others in Britain Morphews volunteered to serve during World War I. Some had joined the British ARMY and Navy prior to the start of the war. The Morphews appeared to serve in their regional regiments, Essex, Suffolk, Surrey, London. Some served with the Guards, northern regiments, the Labour Corps, Royal Engineers and the Royal Artillery. Only a few appeared to have joined the Navy. When the Royal Flying Corps came into existence several joined this air arm of the British Forces, which became the Royal Air Force in 1918. Morphews were represented in all ranks through out the armed forces.

Alfred Morphew, 213548, Royal Navy, 1901.
1918 record Alfred is a Stoker petty Officer.
J. Morphew, 341, Trooper, Natal Mounted Rifles, 1902.

Walter William

Ernest Morphew, SS103605, 1906. 1909 Stoker 1st Class, HMS Duncan. 1918 Ernest is recorded as a Stoker 1st Class.

G. Morphew, Major and Honoury Captain, Queens Own (Royal West Kent Regiment), 1906. Record same year as a Lieutenant Colonel in the same regiment.

Edward Maudsley Morphew, Lieutenant Colonel, Royal Army Medical Corp, 1908. 1914 recorded again as a Lieutenant Colonel. 1918 record as a Lieutenant Colonel. The same year recorded as a Colonel at the War Office.

Vyvyan Willard Morphew, M2102012, Sergeant, Army Service Corp, 1908. At this date was an Acting Company Quarter Master Sergeant. 1914 a record as a Warrant Officer 2 (Sergeant Major). 1917 recorded as a Sergeant.

Ralph H. Morphew, J3534, 1909. 1918 record Petty Officer, HMS Excellent.

George Adames Morphew, M5649, 1913. 1916 record Electrical Articifer 3rd Class, HMS Hampshire. Another record dated 1918.

Edward L. Morphew, 240813, Private, Royal West Kent Regiment, 1914.

George Morphew, 314306, Private, South Wales Borderers, 1914. Another record dated 1917.

Edward L. Morphew, 264035, Private, Northumberland Fusilier, 1914.

George E. Morphew, G/27007, Private, Royal Fusiliers, 1914. 1918 record giving the London Regiment. This could still refer to the Royal Fusiliers. Originally formed as the City of London Regiment and this title was still used during WWI.

George Edward Morphew, 60418, Private, Labour Corp, 1914.

Richard A. Morphew, 89510, Sapper, Royal Engineers, 1914.

Ernest Morphew, 201327, Sergeant, Wiltshire Regiment, 1914.

Robert G. Morphew, GS/4/17872, Private, EastSurrey Regiment, 1914. Later record dated 1917.

Robert W. Morphew, 16685, Private, Suffolk Regiment, 1914.

Robert James Morphew, J28374, Able Seaman, 1914. Second record 1918.

T. Morphew, 324, Shoeing, Royal Field Smith Artillery, 1914.

Robert G. Morphew, T/455627, Private, Army Service Corp, 1914.

Thomas Morphew,116812, Private, Army Reserve, 1914.

Samuel Joseph Briggs Morphew,15975, Private, Grenadier Guards 1914. 1916 Corporal. 1919 Acting Sergeant.

Sidney R. Morphew, 5850, Sapper, Royal Engineers, 1914.

Sidney R. Morphew, WR268660, Sapper, Royal engineers, 1914.

George Frederick Morphew, 202822, Private, Nottinghamshire and Derbyshire Regiment, 1914. Record for 1917 giving as a private in the Sherwood Foresters Regiment. The Nottingham and Derbyshire Regiments were amalgamated in 1881 to form the Sherwood Foresters. But retained the older individual names. Today the Sherwood Foresters amalgamated to form the Mercian Regiment.

Ernest Morphew, 204604, Sereant, South Staffordshire Regiment, 1914.

Ernest Morphew, 29013, Guardsman, Grenadier Guards, 1914. Record in 1917 Ernest is a Private, Guardsman.

Arthur Morphew, SS115038, the first record is in 1913. In 1914 he is a Stoker 2nd class on HMS Pathfinder.

HMS Pathfinder was built in 1904. It was a British Scout Cruiser. It was the first ship to be sunk by a self propelled torpedo fired by a submarine. HMS Pathfinder was sunk on September 5th 1914. The torpedo struck midship causing an explosion in the magazine. Out of the 259 crew on 20 survived.

Arthur Morphew appears to have survived the catatrophic sunking of HMS Pathfinder. He is recorded to be on HMS Hogue which was a Cressy Class armoured cruiser on 22nd September 1914 when HMS Hogue was sunk by a U Boat with two of its sister ships. There is a later record of Arthur Morphew, SS 115038 in 1918.

Albert Morphew, 87556, Private, Royal Army Medical Corp 1914.

Alfred Morphew, 55723, Private, Rifle Brigade, 1914.

Alfred Morphew, 70698, Private, Suffolk Regiment, 1914.

Thomas Morphew, 116812, Private, royal Army Medical Corp, 1914.

Thomas Morphew, 37712, Driver, Royal Field Artillery, 1914.

Thomas C. Morphew, 9037, Private, Gloucestershire Regiment, 1914.

Alfred W. Morphew, 18048, Gunner Royal Garrison Artillery, 1914.

Albert Morphew, G/25695, Private, Royal Sussex Regiment, 1914. Another record dated 1918.

Albert E. Morphew, 1715, Sapper, Royal Engineers, 1914.

Charles H. Morphew, 701644, Private, London Regiment, 1914. Record dated 1918. A further record dated 1919.

Charles H. Morphew, 39292, Private Suffolk Regiment, 1914.

Dennis Morphew, R/258016, Private Army Service Corp, 1914.

The Royal Army Service Corps was a corps of the British Army responsible for land, coastal and lake transport, air despatch, barracks administration, the Army Fire Service, staffing headquarters' units.

W. Morphew, 4134, Private, London Regiment, 1914. Later record 1916.

William Morphew, 8906, Private, Royal Defense Corp, 1914.

Albert P. Morphew, 200199, Driver, Royal Field Artillery, 1914.

E. Morphew, 16485, Corporal, South Wales Borderers, 1914. The same year E. Morphew was recorded as a Sergeant. Record in 1918 record as a Corporal and then the same year a Sergeant.

Albert E. Morphew, 534358, Sapper, Royal Engineers, 1914.

William J. Morphew, 17485, Private, Royal Army Pay Corp, 1914.
William G. Morphew, 16157, Private, Somerset Light Infantry, 1914. Later records for 1916 and 1917.
William J. Morphew, 111293, Gunner, Royal Garrison Artillery, 1914. Later record 1918.
William J Norphew, 6040, Private, London Regiment, 1914.
Henry E. G. R. Morphew, 89103, Acting Sergeant, London Regiment, 1914. Second record as being in the Labour Corp.
William L. Morphew, 2393, Royal West Kent Regiment 1914.
William L. Morphew, 240656, Private, Royal West Kent Regiment, 1914.
Herbert Morphew, 6458, Private, London Regiment, 1914.
Herbert Briggs Morphew, 573330, Private, London Regiment, 1914. 1918 recorded as a Rifleman.
William R. Morphew, 234931, Gunner, Royal Horse Artillery, 1914.
H. J. Morphew, G/20467 Private, East Kent Regiment (Buffs), 1914. Other records, Private 1918 and Private 1919.
Henry Morphew, 8575, Driver, Royal Field Artillery, 1914. Later record shows as a Gunner in the Royal Field Artillery.
Joseph G. Morphew, M2/078950, Private, Army Service Corp, 1914.
J. E. Morphew, 2nd Lieutenant, Royal Field artillery, 1914. Second record 1914 Leiutenant. !917 record 2nd Leiutenant Royal Artillery.

James Morphew, 70470, Gunner, Royal Garrison Artillery, 1914.
Joseph John Morphew, 2822 Private, London Regiment, 1914. Second record for 1915.
Leonard James Morphew, 202535, Private, London Regiment, 1914.
Oliver George Morphew, Private Suffolk Regiment, 1914. Second record 1915.
Arthur William Morphew, 17012, Private, Suffolk Regiment, 1914. Later record in 1915.
R. Morphew, 12967, Private, Essex regiment, 1914.
Bertie George Morphew, 8919, Private, Essex Regiment, 1915.
W. Morphew, Royal Engineers, 1915.
Reginald Morphew, Temporary Lieutenant, Royal Naval Volunteer, 1915. 1916 recorded as a Lieutenant. 1918 joined reserve.
Frank Morphew, 15182, Private, Suffolk Regiment, 1915.
R. W. Morphew, 16685, Private, Suffolk Regiment, 1916, second record for 1916.
J. H. Morphew, 5228, Royal Air Force, 1916. 1918 Air Mechanic 1st Class.
R. J. Morphew, 56169, Private, Canadian Infantry, 1916. Two other records dated 1916
R. H. Morphew, 89510, Sapper, Royal Engineers, 1916.
H. E. G. Morphew, 3487 Sergeant, London Regiment, 1916.
J. J. Morphew, Private, London Regiment, 1916

R. Morphew, 17872, Private, East Surrey Regiment, 1917. Second record for 1917, another record for 1917.
Edwin Oakenfull Morphew, M26045, 1917.
A.S. Morphew, 30386, Private, Essex Regiment, 1917. There is also a later record in 1919.
J. Morphew, 70470, Gunner, Royal Garrison, Artillery, 1917.
William E Morphew, LZ7097, Able Seaman, Royal Naval Volunteer Reserve, 1917. Later record 1918.
Morphew, P/53987, Air Mechanic 3rd class, Royal Flying Corp, 1918.
H.E. Morphew, 276087, Royal Airforce, 1918.
A.W. Morphew, 121007, Royal Air Force, 1918.
Bertie Morphew, 23484, Private, Suffolk Regiment, 1918. Another record 1918 Betie is a Lance Corporal.
Frederick A. Morphew, 4195, Private (Guardsman), Welsh Guards, 1918.
W. Morphew, 701360, Private, London Regiment, 1918.

Morphew military service in United Kingdom armed forces, post 1919

William Morphew, Sergeant, West Yorkshire Regiment, 1925.
G. M. T. Morphew, Lieutenant, Royal Horse Artillery, 1930. Record dated 1930 as being in the Royal Regiment of Artillery.
1938 record, Captain, Royal Regiment of Artillery. 1941 records gives rank as Captain Royal Regiment of artillery then as a Major at the War Office. 1944 record

records as a major in Royal Regiment of Artillery then in the same year as a Captain in Royal Artillery. 1945 record shows as an Acting Colonel. 1950 record shows as a Leiutenant Colonel in the Royal Artillery. In 1953 as a Colonel on active list.
James Frederick Morphew, 553150, Royal Air Force, 1934.
N. H. J. Morphew, 745115, Gunner, Royal Artillery, 1935.
A.J. Morphew, D/22776, Royal Air Force, 1937.
L. P. Morphew, 749221, Royal Air Force, 1937. 1945 record shows as being a Sergeant in 334 Wing.
The 334 Wing was a Mosquito Wing carrying out Recconnaisance for Operation OverLord.
William Thomas Morphew, 621329, Royal Air Force, 1938.
James Gordon Morphew, 64088, Royal Air Force, 1938.
Cyril George Morphew, 1183023, Royal Air Force, 1940.
S. C. Morphew, 545520, Private, Auxiliary Military Pioneer Corp, 1940. 2nd record 1940 giving the Royal Armoured Corp.
Jack Basil Morphew, 1150786, Royal Air Force, 1940.
Henry James Morphew, 1295531, Royal Air Force, 1940.
John Albert Morphew, 116228, Royal Air Force, 1940.
George Victor Morphew, 905717, Royal Air Force, 1940.

Alfred Rowland Morphew, 1470749, Royal Air Force, 1941.
Donald Norris Morphew, 1646943, Royal Air Force, 1941.
Kathleen Hylda Morphew, 2025117, Royal Air Force, 1941.
Doris Vera Morphew, 2020961, Royal Air Force, 1941.
Percival Lawrence Morphew , DR144, Private, Hong Kong Volunteer Defence Corp, 1941.
The Hong Kong Volunteer Defence Corp, (Royal Hong Kong Regiment, The Volunteers) was a local auxiliary militia. In 1941 the Hong Kong Volunteer Defence Force along side British, Canadian and Indian troops in the defence of Hong Kong against an over welming Japanese attack. Hong Kong was surrendered to the Japanese who occupied the territory. Those who defended Hong Kong were taken as prisoners of war and held in two camps.
Hope Morphew, 109177, Nurse, Registered Nurse, 1941.
Geoffrey Leonard Morphew, 1626118, Royal Air Force, 1941. Record dated 1945 as a Sergeant (Pilot), Royal Air Force Volunteer Reserve.
Edward Frank Morphew, 1486990, Sergeant, Royal Artillery, 1942. Record for the same year Battery Quarter Master Sergeant.
Leonard James Morphew, 1865813, Royal Air Force, 1942.
J. Morphew, Captain, South African Air Force, 1942.
E. F. Morphew, 1486990, War Substansive Sergeant, Royal Artillery, 1943. Second record in 1945.

Peter Thomas Bert Morphew, 3038792, Royal air Force, 1943.

Stanley John Morphew, 1893019, Royal Air Force, 1943.

B. J. E, Morphew, 320057, 2nd Lieutenant, Suffolk Regiment, 1944. 1950 recorded as a Captain.

Richard Leslie Morphew, 14267303, Gunner, Royal Artillery, 1944. Another record dated 1944. Two records dated 1945.

Jeffrey Morphew, 102701, Captain, 1944.

Brian Ray Morphew, 587394, Royal Air Force, 1944.

Mrs H. Morphew, Sister, Queen Alexandras Imperial, Military Nursing Service, 1944.

T. J. Morphew, 83063, Gunner, Royal Artillery, 1944.

Kenneth Victor Morphew, 7958625, Trooper, 144 Regiment, 1944. Record for the same year gives the regiment as the Royal Armoured Corp.
The 144 Regiment was originally a company of the East Lancashire Regiment. After the fall of France veterans of the British Expeditionary Force joined the East Lancashire regiment and was made the 8th East Lancashire Battalion. This regiment originally used Churchill tanks but changed over to Sherman tanks and later reverted to Churchill tanks. For the D Day landing they were given Shermans. The 144 East Lancashire Regiment saw continuous action after landing on D Day.

D. J. Morphew, 2041607, Sergeant, Royal Field Artillery, 1945.

Thomas Charles F. Morphew, PKX90282, Mechanic 1st Class, HMS Berwick, 1945.

D. N. Morphew, Pilot Officer, Accountant Branch, 1945.

G. L. Morphew, Sergeant, Royal Air Force, 1945
Frederick James Morphew, 4117483, Royal Air Force, 1946.
A. E. Morphew, 2072185, Corporal, Royal Engineers, 1946.
J. E. Morphew, 420365, Private, Royal Electrical and Mechanical Engineers, 1946.
Victor Everett Morffew, N219089, Private, Australian Army Intelligence Corp, 1946
Russell Nelson Morphew, 3104806, Royal Air Force, 1946
Brian Morphew, 4175334, Royal Air Force, 1946.
E. T. C. Morphew, Civilian 1947.
Leslie John Morphew, 2385392, Royal Air Force, 1947.
Raymond Morphew, 2398767, Royal Air Force, 1948.

American Morphews

At the start of the century Morphews lived mostly down the Eastern Sea Board. From the Northern States down to Texas.

After WWII Citizens' Councils were formed. The first ones were formed in 1954 in Indianola, Mississippi, to resist integration. By March 1955, 167 Citizens' Councils were reported in Mississippi; these were loosely affiliated into a state organisation, Richard D Morphew, (Dick Morphew) was the public relations director for the Citizens Councils. In 1955, the state organisation began producing fifteen-minute weekly films under the name Citizens' Council Forum Films. These films consisted of interviews by the producer, Dick Morphew with American and foreign conservatives and were shown on local television stations throughout the country. The programs were created to persuade public opinion on two main issues, integration and communism.

In the early 1960s Dick Morphew moved to Washington where he could have wider access to politicians. This was at the time when the US Civil Rights Bill was going through Congress. Dick Morphew's show broadcaste debates about the bill where there were many arguments. Dick Morphew appeared to oppose the Civil rights Bill.

After the passage of the civil rights bill in 1964 Dick Morphew's show held debates on the Private Property Rights Bill. Dick Morphew discussed with Walter Rogers, a Democrat Congressman from Texas how this Private Property Bill would clash with the regulation of natural gas. This became known as the 'Tidelands issue'. Dick Morphew argued on the 'Tidelands Issue' saying it allowed the Federal Government to regulate the price of natural gas under the 1938 Natural Gas Act. The Southern gas producing states wanted to change the regulation to allow states to regulate their own prices.

When San Francisco was rebuilt after the earth quacke a street was named Morphew Street. This is in the San Raphael area by the canal and just before the Golden Gate crossing San Francisco Bay.

Morphews can be found across America but are mainly in the eastern states.

Leland Morphews: born 1903, parents Marion H. Morphew and Celia Ann Lee Morphew.

Ruth Edna Morphew: born 1905, parents Marion H. Morphew and Celia Ann Lee Morphew.

Elsie Morphew: born 1907, parents Marion H. Morphew and Celia Ann Lee Morphew.

Mortan Field Morphew: born 1908, parents Marion H. Morphew and Celia Ann Lee Morphew.

Ester Mabel Morphew: born 1909.

Morphews who served in American Armed Forces in WWI

America entered World War One after a German submarine sank the British ocean liner 'Lusitania' on May 7, 1915. More than 120 U.S. citizens died provoking outrage in the U.S. In 1917, Germany's attacks on American ships and its attempts to meddle in U.S.-Mexican relations drew the U.S. into the war on the side of the Allies. The United States declared war on Germany on April 6, 1917 and sent more than a million troops to Europe.

Harley G. Morphew, born 1895.
Melvin Franklin Morphew, born 1882.
Hubert Lee Morphew, born 1882.
George Augustus Morphew, born 1883.
Vestal Harold Morphew, born 1899.
Chas William Morphew, born 1884 Woodward County, Oklahoma.
James Blain Morphew, born 1900. Dallas County, Texas.
Robert Ellis Morphew, born 1900.
David Montgomery Morphew, born 1879 Pike County, Arkansas.
James Radford Morphew, born 1888 Hunt County, Texas.
Ory Morphew, born 1888.
Eden Lewis Morphew, born 1876.
Eugene Belle Morphew, born 1883.

Roscoe G. Morphew, born 1891 Hopins County, Texas.
Howard Hutchinson Morphew, born 1900 Floyd County, Iowa.
John Arthur Morphew, born 1881.
George Addison Morphew, born 1899.
Henry Elis Morphew, born 1893.
Rob Morphew, resident Kentucky.
Lee Louie Morphew, resident Seminole County, Oklahoma.
Burr Whitten Morphew, resident Humboldt County, California.
Fred James Morphew, resident Butler County, Kansas.
Hershal Morphew, resident Putnam County.
Elihugh Morphew, resident Polk County, Arkansas.
Homer Carlos Morphew, resident Hendricks County, Indiana.
Lucius Morphew, resident Bowie County, Texas.
William Morphew, resident Becker County, Minnesota.
Chester Morphew, resident Saline County, Arkansas.
Thomas Wesley Morphew, resident Butler County, Kentucky.
Norman Morphew, resident Hodgeman County, Kansas.
Leonard Lorra Morphew, resident Putnam County, Indiana.
Jesse B. Morphew, resident Pike County, Arkansas.
Joseph Enos Morphew, resident Sebastian County, Arkansas.

Frank B. Morphew, resident McDonnell County, North Carolina.
William Washington Morphew, resident Duval, Florida.
Re- enlisted 1934 until 1948.
James R. Morphew, resident Butler County, Kentucky.
Claude Leslie Morphew, resident Hamilton, Tennessee.
Albert J. Morphew, resident Sevier County,
Arkansas.Frank Morphew, resident Bowie County, Texas.
Obie B. Morphew, resident Bowie County, Texas.
Ollie Morphew, resident Pottawatomie County, Oklahoma.
Henry Elis Morphew, resident Comanche County, Texas.
Albert Humphry Morphew, resident Cottonwood County, Minnesota.
Robert Morphew, resident Butler County, Kentucky.
Robert Benjamin Morphew, resident Walker County, Alabama.
Grady Morphew, resident Pike County, Arkansas.
John Earl Morphew, resident Pottawatomic County, Oklahoma.
Elbert Richard Morphew, resident Hamilton, Tennessee.
Harley G. Morphew, resident Wayne, Michigan.
Alta Forest Morphew, resident Hendricks County, Indiana.
Virgil R. Morphew, resident Lee County, Iowa.

Marion C. Morphew, resident Dubuque, Iowa.
Clarence O. Morphew, resident Butler county, Kentucky.
Simon Lewis Morphew, resident Butler county, Kentucky.
Lorin J. Morphew, resident Jasper, Missouri.
Thomas Allen Morphew, resident Lewis County, Missouri.
Herbert Morphew, resident Pike County, Arkansas.
Samuel H. Morphew, resident Creek County, Oklahoma.
Chas Plesant Morphew, resident Hamilton County, Tennessee.
Thomas A. J. Morphew, resident Webster County, Louisiana.
Ory Morphew, resident Cerro Gordo County, Iowa.
Albert J. Morphew, resident Pike County, Arkansas.
Sherman Morphew, resident Pike County, Arkansas.
Alla Morphew.
Hershal Morphew, resident Putnam County, Tennessee.
Dennie Birdie Morphew, residentSebastian County, Arkansas.
Myrtle Nettie Morphew.
William Morphew, resident Becker County, Minnesota.
Walter Edmund Morphew, resident Cottonwood County, Minnesota.
Clarence Everett Morphew, resident Davidson, Tennessee.

Herbert Austin Morphew, resident Putnam County, Indiana.
Robert Orester Morphew, resident Hendricks County, Indiana.
John Riley Morphew, resident Dubuque, Iowa.
Area Athel Morphew, resident Butler County, Kentucky.
Melvin Franklin Morphew, resident Madison County, Arkansas.
Orville Delane Morphew, resident Hendricks County, Indiana.
John Arthur Morphew, resident Wayne, Michigan.
George Addison Morphew, resident Pottawatomic County Oklahoma.
Burnie Matt Morphew, resident Pope County, Arkansas.
Frank Bryan Morphew, resident Virginia.
Bridget Morphew.
Paul Sterges Morphew, resident Floyd County, Iowa.
Silas Prince Morphew, resident Pike County, Arkansas.
Albert J. Morphew, resident sevier County, Arkansas.
Marion H. Morphew, resident Blue earth county, Minnesota.
Vestal Harold Morphew, resident Hendricks County, Indiana.
John William Morphew, resident Essex, Massachusetts.
Albert Humphrey Morphew, resident Cottonwood County, Minnesota.
George Morphew, resident Warren County, Kentucky.

Grady Morphew, resident Pike County, Arkansas.
Linard Morphew, resident Putnam County, Tennessee.
Annie Morphew.
Levy Thomas Morphew, resident Bowie County, Texas.
Virgil Burnice Morphew, resident Clinton County, Indiana.
Ollie Wallace Morphew, resident Floyd County, Iowa.
William Elza Morphew, resident Marion, Indiana.
Earl Robert Morphew, resident Graham County, Kansas.
Alta Forest Morphew, resident Hendricks County, Indiana.
Ella Morphew.
Fannie I. Morphew.
Charles Franklin Morphew, resident Douglas, Nebraska.
Virgil R. Morphew, resident Lee County, Iowa.
Lorin J. Morphew, resident Jasper, Missouri.
Thomas Allen Morphew, resident Lewis County, Missouri.
Robert Edward Morphew, resident Todd County, Kentucky.

Morphews who served in American armed forces - post 1919

Robert C. Morphew, enlisted army 1939, born 1854.
James C. Morphew, enlisted army 1940, born 1919.
Herman O. Morphew, enlisted army 1940, born 1921.

Eugene F. Morphew, enlisted army 1940, born 1885.
James B. Morphew, enlisted army 1940, born 1922.
Walter L. Morphew, enlisted army 1941, born 1918.
William W. Morphew, enlisted army 1941, born 1915.
Max V. Morphew, enlisted army 1941, born 1913.
Walter L. Morphew, enlisted army 1941, born 1918.
Gordon K. Morphew, enlisted army 1941, born 1918.
William Morphew, enlisted army 1941, born 1918.
Howard I. Morphew, enlisted army 1941. Born 1919.
Bernard C. Morphew, enlisted army 1941, born 1920.
Bryon L. Morphew, enlisted army 1941, born 1921.
Noble D. Morphew, enlisted army 1941, born 1918.
Gordon S. Morphew, enlisted army 1941, born 1921.
Orville Morphew, enlisted army 1942, born 1913.
Floyd W. Morphew, enlisted army 1942, born 1912.
Herbert E. Morphew, enlisted army 1942, born 1913.
Thomas W. Morphew, enlisted army 1942, born 1921.
Roy E. Morphew, enlisted army 1942, born 1921
O. B. Jr. Morphew, enlisted army 1942, born 1914.
John W. Morphew, enlisted army 1942, born 1918.
Leand R. Morphew, enlisted 1942, born 1903.
Virla Morphew, enlisted army 1942, born 1902.
William E. Morphew, enlisted army 1942, born 1922.
Olen D. Morphew, enlisted army 1942, born 1912.
Marion C. Morphew, enlisted army 1942, born 1920.
Paul E. Morphew, enlisted army 1942, born 1923.
Arthur L. Morphew, enlisted army 1942, born 1907.
Kenneth L. Morphew, enlisted army 1942, born 1920.
Orval S. Morphew, enlisted army 1942, born 1918.

Harlie Morphew, enlisted army 1942, born 1910.
Keith L. Morphew, enlisted army 1942, born 1917.
Ennis V. Morphew, enlisted army 1942, born 1823.
Marvin E. Morphew, enlisted army 1943, born 1924.
James A. Morphew, enlisted army 1943, born 1918.
Lawrence E. Morphew, enlisted army 1943, born 1923.
James H. Morphew, enlisted army 1943, born 1923.
Ralph W. Morphew, enlisted army 1944, born 1912.
Hunter B. Morphew, enlisted army 1944, born 1912.
James A. Morphew, enlisted army 1944, born 1920.
Raymond Morphew, enlisted army1944, born 1925
Dolphus Morphew, enlisted army 1945, born 1913.
Glen T. Morphew, enlisted army 1945, born 1928.
Roy E. Morphew, enlisted army 1945, born 1919.
Harry K. Morphew, enlisted army 1945, born 1926
Billie J. Morphew, enlisted army 1946. Born 1926.
Billy G. Morphew, enlisted army 1946, born 1928.
William R. Morphew, enlisted army 1946, born 1926.
Leon Morphew, enlisted army 1946, born 1926.

James E. Morphew served in Korea and died in 1952.

Canadian Morphews

In the early 20th Century Ontario and Quebec vied for prominence in Canada. English speaking (Lambton), Toronto Ontario became the main industrial centre. As the population grew in Lambton so did the suburbs until Lambton became Toronto.

Industry grew in Toronto along with the Westward migration to British Columbia along the Canadian Pacific railroad.

The early records of Morphews in Canada in the 1911 census are recorded mainly in Ontario.

Joseph Morphew; Renfrew.
Richard Morphew; Peel.
Arthur Morphew; born 1904, 1911 census living Renfrew.
Elsie Morphew; born 1907, 1911 census living at Renfrew.
Esther Morphew; born 1909, 1911 census living at Renfrew.

1921 census shows majority of Morphews living in Lambton, Ontario and just two living in Manitoba.

Charles Morphew; Winnipeg, Manitoba.
Christina Morphew; Manitoba.
Jack Morphew; Lambton, Ontario.
Allen Morphew; Lambton, Ontario.
Lillian Morphew; Lambton, Ontario.
George Morphew; Lambton, Ontario.
Jesie Morphew; Lambton, Ontario.
Earnest Morphew; Lambton, Ontario.

Charles Morphew; Lambton, Ontario.
Alfred Morphew; Lambton, Ontario.
Florence Morphew.
Lillie E. May Morphew, Lambton, Ontario.
Brian Morphew, Ontario.
Andrew Francis Morphew, born 1976, Ontario
Graham Roy Morphew, born 1973, Ontario.
Arthur Frederick Morphew, Lambton, Ontario.
Ernest Morphew; Lambton, Ontario.
Josa Morphew; Lambton, Ontario.
William Morphew; Lambton, Ontario.
The 1935 census shows seven records, again in Ontario and Manitoba.
Mr Charles Morphew; Manitoba
Charles F. Morphew; Manitoba.
George Morphew; Lambton, Ontario.
Mrs Alfred James Morphew; Lambton Ontario.
William Morphew; Lambton, Ontario.
Mrs Ernest Morphew; Lambton, Ontario.
During the 1940s the census records showed that Morphews were predominantly living in Ontario. Two Morphews are recorded living in Manitoba and three records of Morphews in Quebec
Miss Margaret Morphew; Manitoba
Mrs Christine Morphew; Manitoba
Charles Morphew; Quebec
Mrs C. Morphew; Quebec
Chae Morphew; Quebec
During the 1950s we find most Morphews living in Ontario. Census records show five records in Quebec, 2 in Alberta and one in Manitoba.

Mrs Marion Morphew: Quebec, 1957 census
Joan Morphew; Quebec, 1957 census
Mrs Marion Morphew: Quebec, 1958 census
Charles Morphew; Quebec, 1957 census
Charles Morphew; Quebec, 1958 census
Doreen Morphew; City Alberta, 1958 census.
William John Morphew, Lambton, Ontario.
Fred Morphew; City Alberta, 1958 census
Christina Morphew; Manitoba, 1953 census.
In the 1960s again we find most Morphews living in Ontario (34) but none living in Manitoba.
Mrs Doreen Morphew; Alberta, 1968 census.
Fred Morphew; Alberta, 1968 census
Ron Morphew; Alberta, 1968 census
Ella Morphew; Alberta, 1963 census
Doreen Morphew; Alberta, 1965 census
Miss Joan Morphew; Quebec, 195 census
Mrs M. Morphew; Quebec, 1968 census.
Mrs Marian Morphew; Quebec, 1963 census
Mrs Marian Morphew; Quebec, 1965 census.
Charles Morphew; Quebec, 1963 census.
Charles Morphew; Quebec, 1965 census
Mr Chas Morphew; Quebec, 1963 census
In the 1970s records nearly all of the Morphews lived in Alberta. Just one lived in Alberta, a Frederick Morphew.

Morphews who served in Canadian armed forces during WWI.

Canadians served through out World War One. Once Britain declared war so did Britains Colonies and Dominions.

The first major battle the Canadians fought in was the Second Battle Ypres.
Then at Beaumont Hamel, Passchendaele and the Hundred Days Campaign.

Leighton Leslie Morphew, Canadian Expeditionary Force, died 1917. *[148 469 Private 78th BN 1916]*
Albert Joseph Morphew, Canadian Expeditionary Force.
Charles Morphew, Canadian Expeditionary Force.
Richard James Morphew, Canadian Expeditionary Force. *[56169 Private 1915 19th BN]*
Earnest Morphew, Canadian Expeditionary Force.
Mrs Violet Morphew.
L. L. Morphew, Canadian Expeditionary Force, died 1917.
John Morphew, Canadian Expeditionary Force.
Ellen Rosa Morphew, Canadian Expeditionary Force.
Percy Lawrence Morphew, died 1917.
Joseph Morphew, Canadian Expeditionary Force.

[Alfred James Morphew 90926 corporal Canadian field Artillery 1915]

Morphews who served in Canadian Armed Forces during WWII.
Edward Frank Morphew, Prisoner of War
Jas Morphew, Prisoner of War
Edward Frank Morphew, Prisoner of War.
J. Morphew, Prisoner of War.
Percy L. Morphew, Prisoner of War, died 1942.
R. L. Morphew, Prisoner of War.
L. Morphew.

Australian Morphew's

After World War Two the Australian Government encouraged British nationals to emigrate to Australia. Many took up the offer.
The majority seemed to settle on the east coast in New South Wales and Queensland.

Hilda Rose Morphew, Queensland.
Minnie Bianche Morphew, Queensland.
Alfred Morphew.
Harry A. Morphew.
Daisy Maude Morphew, New South Wales.
Claude A. Morphew, New South Wales.
Agnes Amelia Morphew.
Harold E. Morphew, New South Wales.
Harry A. Morphew.
Liliah E. H. Morphew, New South Wales.
Reginald J. Morphew, New South Wales.
Alfred Morphew.
Horace A. Morphew, New South Wales.
Frank W. Morphew, New South Wales.
Hilda M. Morphew, New South Wales.
Irene E. Morphew, New South Wales.
Eva Blanche Morphew, New South Wales.
Mark Morphew, Queensland.
Daisy Celeste Morphew, born 1999.
Maria Morphew.
Phillip Morphew.
Christina Fraser Morphew, born 1901.
Alfred Hatton Morphew.

Morphews who served in the Australian Army pre 1919

Australians served in a number of campaigns in World War One, most notably on the Gallipoli Peninsula. The ANZAC forces fought in the Somme, Battle of Pozieres, The First and Second battle of Bullecourt, at the battle of Beersheba in Palestine, Villers-Bretonneux, Battle of Amiens, Mont St. Quentin. Also at Megiddo in Palestine.

W.G. Morphew
F. Morphew.
Herbert Morphew
J. E. Morphew.
Joseph John Morphew.
Thomas Morphew.
William George Morphew.
G. E Morphew.
Albert Morphew
Alfred Morphew.
George Edmund Morphew.
Harry Archibald Morphew.
Ethel Mary Morphew.
Sidney R. Morphew.
Henry Morphew.
B. G. Morphew.
William Leslie Morphew.
H. J. Morphew.
Arthur Morphew, died 1914.
William Robert Morphew.
R. H. Morphew.
E. M. Morphew.
Edward Leonard Morphew.

Frederick A. Morphew.
Samuel L. B. Morphew.
T. B. Morphew.
T. C. MorphewHenry E. G. K. Morphew.
Frederick Thomas Morphew.
A. E. Morphew.
William Thomas Morphew.
Leonard James Morphew.
Arthur William Morphew.
Bertie Alfred Morphew
Ernest Morphew
George Frederick Morphew.
R. Morphew.
B. G. Morphew.
Thomas C. Morphew.
William Morphew.
Herbert Briggs died 1918.
W. Morphew.
Charles Henry Morphew.
Oliver George Morphew
Vyvyan Willard Morphew.
Chas Henry Morphew.
AlbertPeter Morphew.
John Merchant Morphew, died 1917.
Herbert J. Morphew, Resident of Bay of Plenty, New Zealand.

Morphews who served in Australian Army in War II

Eliza Dorothea Morphew.
Edward Frank Morphew, POW.
J. Morphew, POW.
Percy Lawrence Morphew, POW died 1942.

Victor Everett Morphew, died 1946.
Sarah Susan Morphew.
Frederick Walter Morphew, POW.
Henry Morphew.
William Weston Morphew.
Josephine Emily Morphew, POW.
Percy William Morphew, POW.
Edward Frank Morphew, POW.
Edward Thomas Morphew, POW.
Leslie Reginald Morphew.
L. Morphew, POW.

Many of these Morphews who serving in the Australian armed forces ended up as Prisoners of War. They were most likely posted in Singapore and were taken prisoner when Singapore fell to the Japanese.

Morffew

London Morffews

Ivy Morffew; born 1900 Fulham
Henry James Morffew; born 1902 Chelsea
Winifred Pheobe Morffew; born 1902 Fulham
Arthur Robert Morffew; born 1904 Chelsea.
George Morffew: married 1904 at Fulham
George William Morffew: born 1905 Chelsea *died 6 Sept 1980 Peckham*
George Morffew: born 1906 Chelsea.
Emma Harriet Morffew; 1908 Chelsea
Annie Alice L. Morffew; born 1909 Chelsea
Frederick Morffew; born 1910 Chelsea
Percival George Morffew; born 1911 Paddington. Military service; service number 744625 in 1937 in Royal Air Force. In 1945 service number is 384598 in the Royal air Force.
Charles R. Morffew; born 1912 Chelsea
George F. Morffew; born 1913 Hanover Square. Married 1946 at Wavering, Suffolk.
Lilly F. Morffew; born 1914 Chelsea
George Charles Morffew; born 1917 Shoretditch. Military service; service number 931913 three records 1940, 1942 and 1943 each as a sergeant in the Raoyal Air Force.
Constance V. Morffew; born 1917 Chelsea
Henry A. Morffew; born 1917 Chelsea
Naomi M. Morffew; born 1919 Shoreditch.
Hilde E. Morffew; born 1922 Shoreditch
Ellie J. Morffew; born 1925 Camberwell

Derek W. J. Morffew; born 1926 Edmonton
John A. Morffew; born 1928 Hanover Sq.
Margaret F. Morffew; born 1930 Kensington
Henry J. Morffew; born 1930 Battersea
Joyce Morffew; born 1930 Chelsea
Stanley A. Morffew; born 1932 Chelsea
George William Morffew; born 1932 Chelsea.
Dorothy Morffew; born 1935 Chelsea.
Patricia A. Morffew; born 1936 Edmonton
Michael J. E. Morffew; born 1941 Battersea
Doreen R. Morffew; born 1945 Camberwell
Beryl A. Morffew; born 1947 Camberwell
Christopher G. Morffew; born 1946 Paddington
Patricia M. Morffew; born 1950 Paddington
David B. Morffew; born 1952 Fulham
Barbara A. Morffew; born 1953 Fulham
James R. Morffew; born 1954 Ealing
Peter G. Morffew; born 1956 Camberwell
Andrew J. Morffew; born 1957 Fulham
Alan L. Morffew; born 1959 Camberwell
Carol A. Morffew; born 1960 Camberwell
Tracy R. Morffew; born 1961 Ealing
Thomas Morffew; born 1978 Ealing
Claire Lianne Morffew; born 1984 Hounslow
Jack David Morffew; born 1999 Hammersmith

Surrey Morffews

Frederick R. J. Morffew; born 1905 Richmond
Frederick G. Morffew; born 1927 Richmond
Eileen R. Morffew; born 1935 Richmond upon Thames. Married 1975
Stephen Morffew; born 1947 Surrey North Western
Pamela A. Morffew; born 1949 Surrey Northern
Pamela Jean Morffew; born 1969 Kingston on Thames
Kelly Louise Morffew; born 1980 Kingston on Thames
Lindsey Anne Morffew; born 1983 Surrey North West
Laura Jeanne Morffew; born 1987 Surrey North Western
Sophie Danielle Morffew; born 1990 Surrey North Western.
Oliver James C. Morffew; born 1992 Kingston upon Thames.

Essex Morffews

Michael J. Morffew; born 1964 Harlow
Rhiannon Sue Morffew; born 1997 Harlow
Briony Ann Morffew; born 2000 Harlow

Berkshire Morffews

Robert C. Morffew; born 1943 Windsor
Simon M. Morffew; born 1963 Windsor

Sussex Morffews
Alan G. Morffew; born 1946 Lothingland
Sarah J. Morffew; born 1965 Worthing

Kent Morffews
Grant William R. Morffew; born 1968 Tonbridge

Hampshire Morffews
Doris Morffew: born 1908 Basingstoke, died 1993
Stephen James Morffew: born 1985 Winchester
Gareth Michael Morffew: born 1988 Isle of Wight

Warwickshire Morffews
Tasha Ivy Morffew; born 1992 Birmingham

Glamorganshire Morffews
Catherine Anne Morffew; born 1990 Swansea
Harley Elizabeth Morffew; born 1993 Swansea.

Morffews in Holland
Doreen Morffew: born in Dulwich in 1945.
Zoe Heukels Morffew: Parents Nicole Heukels and Doreen Morffew.

Arthur John

Morffew military service in the United Kingdom armed forces, pre 1919

George H. Morffew, 2132, Private, London Regiment, 1914.

A. J. Morffew, 408417, Royal Air Force, 1914. Two other records. Air Mechanic 3rd Class, 1918. Air Mechanic 2nd Class 1918.

Arthur Morffew, 15718, Private, London Regiment, 1914.

George H. Morffew, 205896, Private, London Regiment, 1914. — *London Regt 2132 later*

Frederick George Morffew, 249235, Private Labour Corp, Not medically fit for enlistment, deaf. Two other entries for 1917, Private, Labour Corp, accepted for service. Serving on the fron line in 301st Labour Company. Died during a barrage.

W. W. Morffew, 31492, Royal Air Force, 1916. Second record dated 1918 as a Private.

W. W. Morffew, 31492, Royal Air Force, 1916. A second record dated 1918.

Henry James Morffew, 98698, Driver, Royal Field Artillery, 1914. Second record dated 1917.

W. K. Morffew, 37808, Private, Suffolk Regiment, 1914. Second record dated 1918 in the Cambridgeshire Regiment.

William   *Born 1885*

Morffew military service in the United Kingdom armed forces post 1919

P. G. Morffew, 744625, Royal Air Force, 1937.

George Charles Morffew, 931913, Royal Air Force, 1940. Four further records. 1942 Sergeant, 1942 Sergeant RAF Bourn, 1942 Royal Air Force Volunteer Reserve, 1943 Sergeant Royal Air Force.

[handwritten: DoB 1905]

George William Morffew, Royal Engineers. *[handwritten: 2367964]*

Percival George Morffew, 384598, Royal Air Force, 1945.

John Arthur Morffew, 3081931, Royal Air Force, 1946.

Australian Morffews

In the 20th century Morffews live mainly in Eastern Australia, in particular Victoria.

Henrietta Josine Morffew: born 1912 Ballarat Victoria.
Douglas Morffew: born 1923 Victoria, died 1974.
Elizabeth Florence Morffew: married 1925 in Victoria.
Ettie Josephine Morffew: born 1913 Victoria, Married 1933. died 1980.
Eva Morffew: record in 1933 of a petty session (minor crime), Victoria.
Edna Rose Morffew: died 1995 Victoria.

[Handwritten notes:]

Son in law ✓
Frederick Laurence moffew
borne South Melbourne Victoria
enlisted Melbourne
Australian Imperial Force

sibling Collis moffew

_____

Arthur James Morffew 44
Melbourne Australian Imperial Force

21st Century

Today we find Morphew's, Morffews and Maufes through out the world.

Most commonly they are found in Britain living through out the country, especially in those counties the Maufe's originally settled; Sussex, Surrey, Norfolk and Suffolk.

Those with Maufe, Morphew and Morffew name are found through out America and Canada. In each country they are predominantly on the Eastern Sea Board.

Morphews in Australia are predominantly found on the Eastern coast of Australia. A telephone directory shows most live in New South Wales, followed by Queensland. Some live in Western Australia and Southern Australia. The name is not common, just as it has not been in previous centuries.

Morffew can be found through out the United Kingdom in Wales, Scotland and of course England where they are in numerous counties but mainly in Southern England.

Morffew's live along the Eastern side of Australia and in Tasmania.

Maufe's live mainly in Southern England but some live in Canada.

Maufe's, Morphew's and Morffews are found in numerous occupations. In the arts there are artists, dancers and photographers.

They can also be found in Engineering, Science and Medicine. They are teachers and lecturers as well as farmers

In Conclusion

The ancestry of the Maufé, Morphew and Morffew is approaching 1000 years. Who would have thought that a name that refered to the Devil or a Demon. Also used as a derogatory term for a Muslim in the Middle Ages would have endured, when other more prominent families in the Middle Ages died out.
The Maufé's started with their holding at Woodford on the River Nene in Northamptonshire and land at Possingworth in Sussex. Later gaining land at Hemington and Armston in Northamptonshire. Chiddingley, Eastbourne, Eastdene, Chalvington, Hoathley, and Hailsham in Sussex. As well as Wooley in Huntingdonshire (Cambridgeshire), also land in Surrey. They faired well for 400 years. They were trusted to help guard the southern approaches in the Sussex Rape of Pevensey and attained standing of minor importance. During the Middle Ages England was embroiled in wars with France and Scotland. Also there were England's internal conflicts with the baron wars where the Maufes showed they could be trusted. But during the 15th century things changed when Henry V invaded France and invited the English to settle in Normandy and France. This is a time when there is very little mention of the Maufe name compared to previous centuries. The Wars of the Roses was a troublesome time for many who owed allegiance to Dukes, Earls and Barons. Many were drawn in to the bloody conflict that dragged on for over thirty years. During this time there were also rebellions. But unlike previous rebellions those of the 15th century included knights, gentry and those of social standing. The most prominent was the Rebellion of the

Duke of Buckingham. The rebellion drew in many from the southern counties, from Kent to Cornwall. Also the counties just north of London.
After Buckinghams Rebellion was suppressed Parliament convened and passed the Act of 1484. Stipulating Individuals who were involved or associated with those involved were to have their land attainted. Also those assumed to be associated in some way or another suffered in a similar way under Richard III Reading through records of those named in this rebellion it is not possible to find either Maufe or Morphew. But because of association it could be that they were affected by the actions of the Lord, Earl or Baron they owed allegiance to.
The Duke of Buckingham held land in many counties, including Sussex, Surrey Huntingdonshire and Norfolk, area's associated with the Maufe's and also later where Morphews are recorded. Maufe's are recorded in the early 16th century but the name seems to die out after this.
The mid 15th century seems to be the time when the Maufe name changed to Morphew. It is difficult to pin point precisely when the name changed in the 15th Century. There is no trace in records of any one with the name Morphew until after the Wars of the Roses. But when we consider that John Howard, The Duke of Norfolk. was given many of the estates previously owned by the Duke of Buckingham including Sussex, Surrey and Huntingdonshire we can speculate that this was the catalyst for the change, combined with the colonisation of Richard III loyal northern supporters coming south after Buckinghams rebellion. We can see a patern of the Maufes in Sussex, Surrey and

Huntingdonshire owing allegiance to The Duke of Norfolk. Under the Parliamentary Act of 1484 the Maufes, along with other's could be moved to where ever dicatated. This could account for the name change with Howard possibly ordering the Northern administrators to change the name to prevent attainted land being taken back. Also under this act those involved in or associated with Buckinghams Rebellion could be moved away from their area of influence. This could account why we find Morphews in Norfolk and Suffolk. Also Morphews cannot be found in Sussex during the 16th century but are living on the fringes of the Weald in Surrey. One place that points to the possible connection with John Howard taking over an estate is at Bletchingley. The Duke of Buckingham held this estate and favoured living at Tonbridge not far away. John Howard very likely received Bletchingley estate and manor. Prior to the 16th century there are no records of Maufes or Morphews living here but in the early part of the 16th Century we find Morphews here.

Also in the 16th century we find Morphews living not far from the Duke of Norfolks estate at Stoke by Nayland, Norfolk.

The problem with changing your name in these times was trying to get your land back if the opportunity arose, or if a pardon was offered. This was evident in the Jack Cade rebellion where there was a pardon offered to those who took part and gave their real name. Some changed their name to try and escape any punishment. Those who did change their name or gave a false name and caught were punished and in some cases executed. The name might have changed to Morphew intentionely or the pronounciation was mis-heard by the Loyal

Northern supporters of Richard III when they were brought south and colonised the Southern Counties. Some one from Northumberland or North Yorkshire could easily mis-understand an accent in the Weald of Sussex. In the 16th and 17th century those in land of the Weald were refered to as "The Wildishers", showing how those living in the Weald were considered.

It could be possible that the Morphew name was a given name or nick name by those who were in the same army as the Maufe. Especially if there were any who had gone on the 1365 Crusade and were lead by Jean de Morphou. The name Mauffee appears in several Medieval documents showing how the transition from Maufe to Mauffee, then to Morfee and to Morphew can easily have taken place over time.

But what ever caused the Maufe name to change to Morphew ~~it has stuck and wa~~s recorded in the Parish Records introduced by Henry VIII in the 16th Century. As the iron industry in the Weald boomed, bringing prosperity Morphew's are coincidentally found in villages not far from where the Maufé's held land. Also Morphews are found in Surrey where the Iron and Green Stone and Fullers Earth was being mined. Grande buildings and palaces were being built during this time such as None Such Pallace and Richmond Palace.

In the 17th Century James I signed a declaration for a colony to be founded in the America's called Virgina. Many were lured with the promise of land and money after working on an indentured contract. It makes you wonder how many of those early Morphews survived the perils and arduous work, to later help populate other colonies and states on the Eastern sea board of

America. Here in America early records have various misspellings. Also some are written as Murphy. But speculation suggests that some of these Murphy's were not of Irish origin but Morphews.

In the 18th Century we find various spellings associated with Morphew in documents. These are Morphen, Murphy, Morphee, Morfee and others.

At the turn of the century the name Morffew appear's in the Parish records in Kingston upon Thames. Some are connected with St. Andrews Church. The big question again is why would Morphew change to Morffew?

Again it suggests mis-spelling in parish records. It might be that some one understood the meaning of the name 'Morphew' as a medical term and decided to change it, or was it changed for them? Again we would never know.

During the 19th century Morffews moved from Kingston to Chelsea and London. Morffews migrated to Australia half way through the century. From Australia Thomas Morffew migrated to Calafornia to set up a dental surgery.

After searching for Maufe in various records over the centuries there does not appear to be any until 1909 the Muff family name was changed to Maufe by deed pole. This seems to have resurrected the Maufe name in Britain.

Today the Maufe name exists in France. Possibly they could be related to Maufe's who went to Normandy and France with Henry V.

In the 21st century we find Maufe's, Morphew's and Morffews living across the United Kingdom and around the globe. Proportionately when compared to people with other names such as Smith, Taylor or Baker there are very few. Maufes, Morphews and Morffews are in a wide range of professions and prominent positions in these professions. Some are directors of companies. Strangely enough we also find Maufes, Morphews and Morffews still living close to where their ancestors lived in the 11th century. Some still own land, farming for a living.

Today the name Morfu is found in Italy, could it have originated from the Normans who travelled south to offer their services to the warring factions. This name can be found in Argentina where Italians were encouraged to migrate and settled in their own communities. Maybe they are related to the Maufe's of the 10th century when Normans travelled south to Italy.

The main aim of this book was to find when the Maufe name changed to Morphew. There are still questions over precisely when this happened but some clarity has been shed on when this might have happened. It appears the Duke of Buckingham, Richard II and John Howard are all partly responsible. *and the possible pronunciation of maufee in contemporary french was it pronounced the same way in the middle ages*

An historical coincidence?

Whilst research this book I came across a peculiar connection between the Maufes and Morphews with the Cressey name. Through history the two names appear together one way or another. This can be construed merely as coincidence or a quirk of fate. It most probably is but I found it strangely interesting how they appeared together over the centuries.

The first connection is in a document from 1235 where William de Cressey, Simon Maufe and other witness's called Henry III to the bench for selling land to pay off his debts.

Another connection between the names was in 1864. J.C. Morphew was the Reverend of Crimplesham in Norfolk. In Crimplesham there are memorials to the Cressey family.

The next connection is peculiarly random. Arthur Morphew served on HMS Hogue in World War One. HMS Hogue was a Cressey class ship.

At this stage is can be considered just coincidence. But during World War One there are further revelations.

W. Morphew, Herbert Morphew, J. J. Morphew and S.W. Cressey all served in the London Regiment.

R. Morphew and J. Cressey served in the East Surrey Regiment.

Another example is of Albert Morphew and Earnest Stanley Creasey served in the Royal Sussex Regiment. It is not clear if all of these individuals were in the same battalion, company or platoon, or even fought in the same battles. Many of the Infantry Regiments in World War One had several battalions.

A later connection is after World War Two. B.J.E. Morphew was a 2nd Lieutenant in the Suffolk Regiment in 1944. In 1950 he is recorded as being a captain. In 1949 L. Cressey was a private in the Suffolk Regiment. It could be possible their paths crossed as some point. Up until 1947 the Suffolk Regiment had two battalions but one was disbanded that year almost ensuring they served at the same time in the same single battalion.
At this point it does make you wonder about all of these coincidences. Is it just fate or is it something deeper.
My own interest in the connection of the Cressey name with Maufes and Morphews stems from my trip around New Zealand in 1987. I spent six months travelling the full length of the country. This included some out of the way places. One of these places was Karamea.
Some one recommended Karamea when I travelled on the bus to West Port. I could have easily gone south, but the temptation to head north to Karamea where the road ended was too great. I walked most of the way and got a lift for the last thirty kilometres or so in a workers truck. These guys advised against staying at the camp site and suggested instead staying at the domain. This is a sort of park area where you could camp.
I was the only person there for the first few days but a car towing a caravan pulled in and a couple set up camp.
Understandably we got chatting and over the few days they were at the Karamea we got to know each other quite well.
At the time their family name, Cressey did not have any significance but after find these historical connections it does feel reality can be stranger than fiction.

By meeting these two at Karamea the Cressey connection is now with the Maufes, Morphews and Morffews.

If the names were Smith, Baker or Taylor it could be purely coincidental because they are so common. Cressey, Maufe, Morphew and Morffew are not at all common names. Looking at the records there are approximately a thousand individuals with all of these names together alive at the same time. The chances of their paths crossing is quite slim.

Having said that I have met another Peter Morffew which was a very strange experience. Yes life is full of coinsidences.

Bibliography

The Wars of the Roses
Charles Ross

Tudor England
John Guy

The Wars of the Roses
Anthony Goodman

**The Wars of the Roses
England's first civil war**
Trevor Royle

The Templars
history and myth
Michael Haag

Oxford English Dictionary (unabridged)
(origins of the surname "Morphew")

English Crusaders
Dansey James Cruikshank
Written 1850

Feudal England: Historical Studies on the XIth and XIIth Centuries
By John Horace Round

Fleuron English surnames: essays
By Mark Antony Lower

Peterborough Abbey 1086-1310
By Edmund King, Professor of History Edmund

Mémoires de la Société linnéenne de Normandie, Volume 1
By Société linnéenne de Normandie

Gods War
Christopher Tyerman

Cyprus: society and culture 1191-1374
By Angel Nikolaou-Konnarē, Christopher David Schabel

The Crusades: a history
By Jonathan Riley-Smith

The Crusades and the military orders: expanding the frontiers of medieval History
By Zsolt Hunyadi, József Laszlovszky, Central European University. Dept. of Medieval Studies

The Medieval Kingdoms of Cyprus and Armenia
By William Stubbs

The Crusades A History of armed pilgrimage and holy war
Geoffrey Hindley

Larousse Encyclopaedia of Ancient and Medieval History

The Black Death
Philip Ziegler

Dictionary of English Surnames

Paper : The Bretons and Normans in England in 1066-1154.
The family fief and the feudal monarchy
KSB Keats - Rohan

The debate of the Norman Conquest
Marjorie Chibnall Manchester University Pre

**Conquest and Colonisation.
The Normans in Britain 1066 – 1100**
Brian Golding

**The Norman Conquest
A New Introduction**
Richard Huscroft

Norman and Anglo-Norman Participation in the Iberian *Reconquista* c.1018 - c.1248
By Lucas Villegas-Aristizábal BA (Hons), MA.
Thesis submitted to the University of Nottingham for the degree of Doctor of Philosophy

The Domesday Quest
Michael Wood BBC books

Normans and their adversaries
Richard P Abels and Bernard S. Bachrach

Society of Norman Italy
G.A. Loud and A. Metcalfe

The English Resistance
The underground war against the Normans
Peter Rex

Norman England
Peter Lane

Race and the origin of American Neoliberalism
Randulph Hohle

Online resources

Planet Murphy
http://www.planetmurphy.org/pagebuild.php?pagebody1=index.html
Extensive information about the Morphew families in America, from the early 18th century to the 20th century. In depth information and detail about movement between various counties and states.

British History on line. Parishes
www.british--history.ac.uk/vch/northants/vol3/pp255-262
www.british-history.ac.uk/rchme/northants/vol1/pp52-54

A History of Cyprus
http://www.kypros.org/Sxetikos/Library/ByzantineChurches/AHistoryofCyprus-5.htm

Merriam-Webster
www.merriam-webster.com/dictionary/cotton

Catholic Encyclopedia
http://www.newadvent.org/cathen/04543c.htm

Morffew Family History
www.gwydir.demon.co.uk/edkins/others/morffew.htm

Zoe Heukels-Morffew & Nils Visser- Huizen, The Netherlands.
http://morpheweb.com/morffew/morffewpartonetext.doc

Georgia health info
http://georgiahealth.info.gov/cms/root

Cyprus
http://fmg.ac/Projects/Medlands/Cyprus /

Full name directory
www.fullnamedirectory.com/page232618.htm

John Morffew's Geneology Research
http://morpheweb.com/morphgenealogy/johnpage1.html

Vassals of the Kingdom of Jerusalem
http://en.wikipedia.org/wiki/Vassals_of_the_Kingdom_of_Jerusalem

Surname DB
www.surnamedb.com

Sussex on line Parish Clerks
www.sussex-opc.org

Unromantic Richard III
https://unromanticrichardiiiblogspot.com/2008/01/second-duke-and-duchess-of-buckingham.html

Intriguing History
www.intriguing-history.com

Medieval Genealogy
www.medievalgenealogy.org.uk

British Battles
www.britishbattles.com

www.britishbattles.com/wars-of-the-roses/battle-of-northampton

www.britishbattles.com/wars-of-the-roses/battle-of-st-albans

https://medievalaccomodation.com/medieval-britain/LMB%20Pages/pages-n-r/buckingham.htm

Battle of Evesham Medieval Festival
www.battleofevesham.co.uk

Exploring Surreys Past
www.exploringsurreyspast.org.uk

Hextalls of Bletchingley in County of Surrey About 1445
https://sites.google.com/site/ukgenealogycom/hextall-s-of-blechingley

Complete listing of Early Virginia immigrants 1623-1666
From book published 1912 by George Cabell Greer.
www.evmedia.com/virginia/

Archaeologia Cantiana Vol 37 19125 Maidstone sector of Duke of Buckinghams Rebellion 1483
Agnes Ethel Conway

Wikipedia
www.wikipedia.org
An extensive resource that has helped on numerous occasions through out this book.

Henry V as Warlord.
https://erenow.net/biographies/henry-v-as-warlord/17.php

Henry III Fine Rolls project
https://finerollshenry3.org.uk/home.html

Gentry Politics of Southern England 1461 – 1485.
With reference to the crisis of 1483.
M.L. Gill
core.ac.uk

Anglo Norman Dictionary
www.anglo-norman.net/gate/

Dictionary of Middle French 1330-1500
www.atilf.fr/dmf

Dictionnaire du Moyen Français
http://www.atilf.fr/dmf.

Dictionnaire L'Ancienne Langue Française
https://archive.org/details/dictionnairedela02godeuoft

A history of British Surnames
Richard McKinley

Discovering Shropshires History
http://search.shropshirehistory.org.uk/

Norman Aristocracy in the Long Eleventh Century. 3 case studies
James Moore

Northamptonshire Record Society. King Stephen and Empress Matilda. The view from Northampton
Edmund King

Bound to Serve; Indentured Servitude in Colonial Virginia, 1624 to 1776.
Penny Howard.
https://kb.gcsu.edu/cgi/viewcontent.cgi?article=1119&context=thecorinthian

The History of English
Luke Mastin
www.thehistoryofenglish.com

Roots Chat
www.rootschat.com

Connected Annals of the manor and family of Perton, Stafford.
Edward A. Hardwicke L.R.L.F.I. inst. F.R.C.I.
Printed 1897

Family Search
www.familysearch.org

Local Histories
www.localhistories.org

British Cavalry Regiments
http://britishcavalryregiments.com

Forces War Records
www.forces-war-records.co.uk

Old Maps
www.old-maps.co.uk

Frances Frith, old maps
www.francisfrith.com

Google Maps

British Listed Buildings
https://britishlistedbuildings.co.uk

Oxford English Dictionary
www.oed.com

Report of the Deputy Keeper of Public. RecordsCalendar Patent Rolls vol 9
Sdrc.lib.uiowa.edu/patentrolls

Calendar of Charters and documents relating to the Abbey of Robertsbridge

The Token Book of St. Saviour, Southwark.
www-personal.umich.edu/~ingram/StSaviour/

Free Reg
www.freereg.org.uk

Geni
www.geni.com

Wiki Tree
www.wikitree.com

British Library
Greek in Tudor England
Micha Lazarus
http://hellenic-institute.uk/research/etheridge/Lazarus/Tudor-Greek.html

Merriam Webster Dictionary
www.merriam-webster.com/

History and Antiquities of Eynesbury and St. Neots in Huntingdonshire, and of st. Neots in county of Cornwall.

Epidemics in Colonial America 1519 – 1787. A Genealogical Perspective
Larisa R. Schumann

Ancestry UK
www.ancestry.co.uk

Sydney Morning Herald
www.smh.com

Sussex Urchatological Collections. Sussex Archaological Society 1894

Other resources
Ordinance Survey Maps

Lonely Colonist Seeks Wife: The Forgotten History of America's First Mail Order Brides
MARCIA ZUG

https://scholarship.law.duke.edu/

The Career of John Howard, Duke of Norfolk 1420-1485
Anne Crawford
Bedford College, University of London
https://core.ac.uk/download/pdf/78865333.pdf

The Speedwell voyage

Tale of Piracy & mutiny in the Eighteenth century

Kenneth Poolman

https://archive.org/details

Other books by Peter G. Morffew

**My Long Journey by Bus, Boat and Train.
A backpackers adventure around India and Sri Lanka.**

Peter Morffew's story of his three month adventure of India and Sri Lanka.
In 1980 Peter travelled the length of India by train, bus and ferry to Sri Lanka.
Peter travelling the full length of India, from the very southern tip to Srinagar in Kashmir in the far north, and Northern Sri Lanka.

Future publications

Peter realises that this publication does not cover everyone, even though he intended it to be as extensive as possible. At some point Peter Morffew is planning to write a 2nd edition with the intention for it to be more comprehensive.
If you wish to forward any information or details of Maufe's, Morphew's or Morffew's to be included in this book please e mail them to the address below.
pmorffew@hotmail.com

places to photograph.

Fifield Bavant ✓
Hemingstone — 1hr 16 mins 57 miles
Woolley — 56 mins 50 miles

{ Kingsthorpe
Northants { Hemington = 1hr 14 mins 61 miles
{ Arnston = 8 mins 3.3 miles
{ Woodford = 24 mins 9.4 miles

Chittingley Sussex
Ripe Sussex
Possingworth Sussex 1hr 37 mins 78.8 miles
Heathrey
Horse eye